THE KEEN CAMPER®

CAMPING WITH KIDS

VOLUME 1

G. EDWARD RIDDLE

SE SEVEN

SOUTHEAST SEVEN
PUBLISHING

The Keen Camper Camping with Kids Volume 1
All Rights Reserved.
Copyright © 2018 G. Edward Riddle

First Edition, First Printing - December 2018

Southeast Seven Publishing
P.O. Box 251108
Plano, TX 75025-1108

http://www.southeastsevenpublishing.com

Paperback ISBN: 978-0-9988716-0-8
Hardback ISBN: 978-0-9988716-1-5

Library of Congress Control Number: 2017917159

PRINTED IN THE UNITED STATES OF AMERICA

TABLE OF CONTENTS

DISCLAIMER

This book contains advice—lots of it in fact. While this advice has worked well for the author, his family, and those he has camped with, it might not work as well (or at all) for you and your family. Therefore, please take the advice in this book as merely things to consider.

Additionally, for anything medical related, please seek the counsel of a trained medical professional when making decisions based on the suggestions provided in this book. If any adverse reactions occur from following any of the guidance in this book, please seek appropriate medical attention immediately.

Neither the author or publisher will be liable for any consequences resulting from following the advice in this book. The decision whether to follow this advice is yours.

Finally, common sense should always prevail. In cases where the author has suggested things that are contrary to what has worked well for you and your family in the past, your experience should take priority.

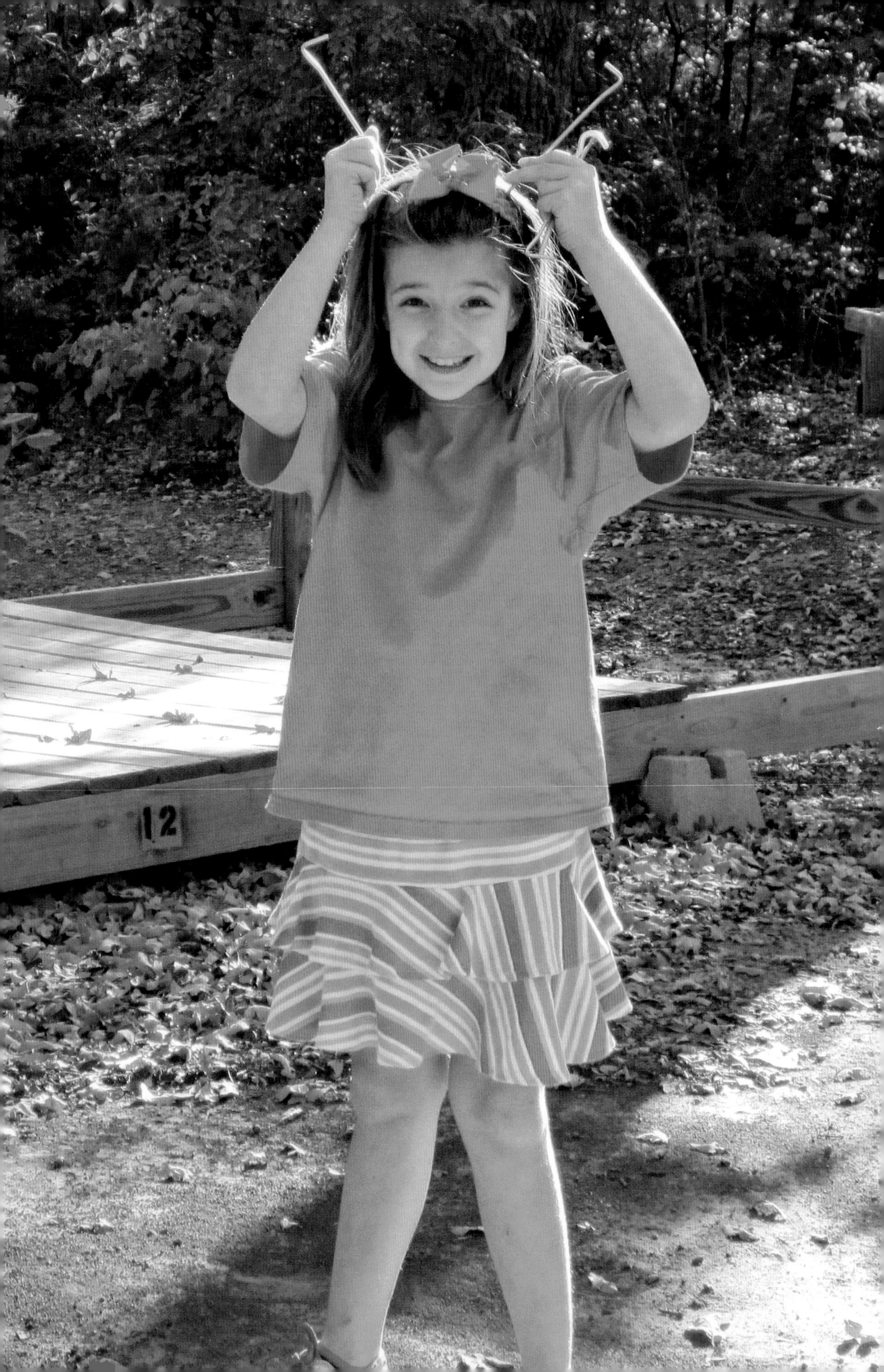
12

CHAPTER 1

INTRODUCTION

Several years back, I realized that most of my friends and acquaintances outside of work (and a good deal of those I knew from work) knew me for being an avid camper. I was someone who genuinely liked the outdoors, knew how to camp, and liked taking others camping—even kids! As I realized this, it started me down the path of thinking, *"Why does everyone think of me in such a passionate light regarding camping?"* While I was successful in several other areas of my life including my career, it was still the realm of camping where I was thought of the most highly. What was I doing differently in my camping hobby that I was obviously not completely replicating elsewhere? Did I just enjoy camping so much that I was giving it 100 percent but not putting an equivalent effort into the other areas of my life? Why did people come to me for advice on camping on such a frequent basis and why did they see me as such an expert in this area? That is certainly not how I saw myself. I thought that if I could boil it down to the nuts and bolts of what was going on, I could apply this secret formula to other areas of my life. What proceeded was a lot of soul searching and introspection over a long period.

What I came to realize surprised me. It turned out it was not my passion for camping. Instead, it was my passion for *helping others enjoy camping*. With camping, my entire focus was helping others to have the absolute best time they could. Knowing that most people who were doing family camping had most likely never done it before, I put a lot of my focus into helping them have a fantastic time. So, at the end of the day, I was not well known as a camper because I loved camping, but instead, because I cared about people and wanted to see them be successful in an area that I just so happened to know something about.

This, in turn, led to this book. My primary objective was to put down on paper all of these helpful hints that I had been sharing with others into a series of books that families new to camping could use. My second goal was that I wanted to extract from these camping experiences what leadership skills I was mastering that could be transferable to other areas in my life. How could I be a more impactful and effective leader to those in my family, the organizations I lead at work, and the non-profit boards I am involved with?

I also wanted the book to be very accessible. I remember standing in line at a juice bar a few years ago waiting for one of their team members to prepare my smoothie. This one specific store had a whole slew of books. I picked up one of them that had an interesting cover. While it was probably a fine book, it was full of page after page of text with almost no pictures and even fewer bulleted lists. I wondered if I was going to have to read all of it before I could utilize the knowledge inside. Do not get me wrong. I think books with lots of words are super . . . for fiction and biographical works, that is. Not for "how-to" books. A few spots over on their bookshelf, I found a book called *The Top 100 Juices*. It had a single page dedicated to each juice. It was a more appropriate style of book for a "how-to" topic. I could easily thumb to the specific section I was interested in, find a juice that interested me, and then read that page. It was a very efficient format for acquiring information.

I wanted to provide a similar concept with this book. For example, take the situation where you are going camping this coming weekend, and you want to cook a meal using a Dutch oven. While you do not have much time to prepare, you still would like to see if you can get it all figured out in time. With this book, you can go directly to the appropriate chapter ("Food & Cooking"), and then thumb through the self-contained sections until you find the information you need. It is that simple.

Also, at the end of each chapter, I have provided an overview of the key leadership skill that was embedded and associated with that aspect of camping. The goal is that after you read that chapter and went camping, you could come home and apply the concepts to other aspects of your life. Areas such as leading your family, working with co-workers, and interacting with your friends. The heart of every chapter is anchored in an unfailing desire to serve others—to help them enjoy something possibly very unfamiliar to them (in this case, camping in the outdoors) in a way that empowers and frees them.

I hope that you enjoy this book and that your family is blessed by your application of it. I know that my family and I have been positively impacted by my shift to be more focused on serving others and to be less focused on myself.

I read somewhere that the purpose of a family is for "teaching." Camping is a marvelous way to teach your family (including both you and your spouse, as well). It has the advantage of being very equalizing since most people are not campers by nature. It also forces you to get outside of your comfort zone, and if done correctly, can help those involved to develop a real sense of accomplishment and self-worth.

Camping allows you to establish or reestablish your role in the family as a leader (and possibly a hero). It also lets you set up situations to help your kids (and possibly your spouse) grow.

A last final preparatory comment. On the Mondays following my weekend campouts, people often ask me, "*Did you have a relaxing time?*" To their surprise, I quite often respond, "*If I wanted to have a relaxing time, I would go by myself.*" While I always make sure to say it very lightheartedly, it is very true. If my family is having a nice time on a campout, I am probably not sitting down that much "relaxing." I would argue that people are asking me the wrong question. The real question is *Did I have a fantastic time*? The answer to that is a resounding "yes." Seeing my spouse relax and my kids having fun in an independent, empowering, non-entertainment-driven-addicted way, is the absolute best.

Just remember . . . It is not about you—it is about *them*.

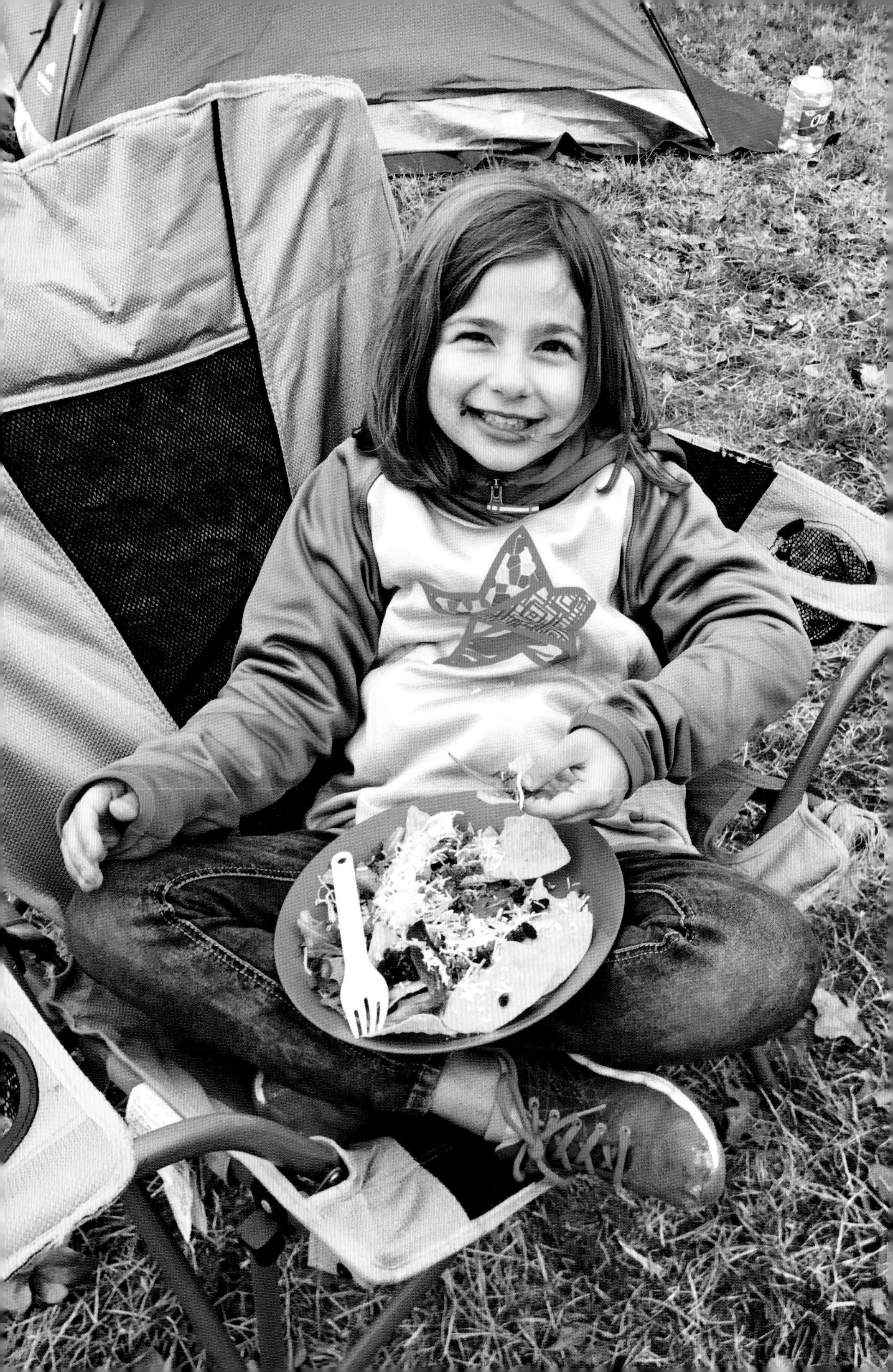

CHAPTER 2

FOOD & COOKING

Food is critical to making or breaking the mood of the campout

Hunger can undoubtedly impact someone's mood. Add to it the additional stress for those new to camping, and you could have some less-than-thrilled campers on your hands. If you then throw in some especially cold and/or wet weather, the moods could be even worse. And if your sleep the night before was less than stellar, some might be thinking about packing everything up and heading home. While this book will cover how to best handle many of the above situations, once your crew is in the middle of them, you will need to try to snap them out of it. A sure-fire method is via food. Good food, and especially *really* good food served warm, can be a real mood changer. And since *really* good food is so often unexpected on a campout, it can have an impact much larger than you would expect.

When I was a Boy Scout, I always looked forward to Mr. Murray's Dutch oven cobbler. No matter how bad of a day it had been or how terrible my patrol's food was, we always had Mr. Murray's hot cobbler to look forward to. It was always a game changer for me. Because of the impact it had on me, whenever I am responsible for meals on a campout, I always make sure Saturday night's dinner is followed by a hot Dutch oven dessert. Period. It always happens. Sometimes, it is a cobbler and other times it is something else. Regardless, my family looks forward to it, enjoys it, and devours it with little to none left afterward.

Cooking is critical for successful camping. Very few campout experiences are as rewarding as preparing a meal outdoors that is of the same caliber as one of your best home-cooked meals. The key is to make sure you are serving high-quality food and have enough of it to completely feed your crew (and maybe a few others that are camping nearby).

As an example, think about how you and your taste buds respond to the following:

Cold Pop-Tarts for breakfast versus ***hot eggs, bacon, toast, and pancakes***

Which sounds better to you? Which one puts you in a better mood? If you want to use campout food to positively impact others, then please consider the following:

- ☀ Have enough food for everyone
- ☀ Buy the highest quality food that you can afford
    - ☼ Grass-fed vs grain-fed meat; organic vs GMO
- ☀ Maintain the appearance of your food
    - ☼ Protect bananas, bread, chips, and produce
- ☀ While eating healthy is important, do not make it too lean
    - ☼ Make sure you have enough fats, carbs, and proteins

Dutch ovens create a unique tradition

Piping hot desserts after a weekend of not-the-best food was always something I looked forward to on my Scout campouts as an 11-year-old. I had never even heard of this wonderful device called a Dutch oven. All that I knew was that cobbler came out of a Dutch oven. And after a weekend of not-so-appetizing Scout-cooked food, the cobbler was all that I could think about, and this Dutch oven was going to provide it to me. It turned out this was a tradition of my specific Boy Scout troop—that the adults always fixed Dutch oven cobbler on Saturday night of the campout. This memory stayed so fondly with me that I quickly made it our Saturday night campout tradition too. Without fail, it is always a big hit.

So what is a Dutch oven? Simply put, it is a cast iron pot with a lid. For camping, there is a special version that has three little legs on the bottom to lift it off the ground and a lid with a large lip for holding coals. Like an oven at home, the Dutch oven works as an actual oven. At home, a heating element heats the air, which is held in by the oven. For a Dutch oven, hot coals placed underneath and on top of the oven heat the cast iron. Cast iron by its very nature evenly distributes the heat. With a Dutch oven, you can cook food in the same manner as a traditional oven.

Dutch ovens vary widely in price from affordable to very expensive. When you buy yours, make sure to get the camping version with three legs and a lip on the lid. If you are only going to own one Dutch oven, I suggest getting a 12-inch wide deep model. After you get your confidence level up, you will probably want to purchase a second one. One for your entrée and one for your dessert. There are even smartphone apps and books that tell you the number of coals you will need for a specific-size Dutch oven to achieve a specific temperature.

While the cost of Dutch ovens tends to be related to the quality and how smooth the cast iron is, the less expensive ones tend to be just fine for camping—especially, if you line them with foil before each use. For cast iron skillets at home where you actually use the patina finish to cook on, the higher quality and cost is worth it. Once again, for campouts the lower cost ones will be perfectly fine—especially, when you are just getting started.

While this is just a brief introduction to Dutch ovens, please find an entire chapter dedicated to Dutch ovens in the second volume of *The Keen Camper Camping with Kids* book series.

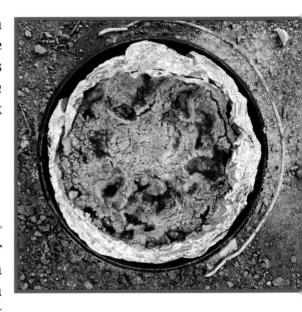

Propane stoves are convenient and simplify your cooking

Instant-on cooking equipment far outweighs any loss of nostalgia by using propane stoves on a camping trip. What is funny about this statement is that for my kids (who are used to Instant Pots, Keurigs, convection ovens, and microwave ovens), propane stoves do conjure up thoughts of camping. To the present generation, camping with propane stoves will someday be their nostalgia.

When I started in Boy Scouts in the mid-1970s, we cooked everything over an open fire. One of our Assistant Scoutmasters had a pop-up camper that he brought on every campout. He and the other adult leaders used it as a home base. One of its neatest features was its propane stove. While we were out cooking our food over open fires, the adults were in there easily cooking eggs, pancakes, and more. Forget the fact that I was only in seventh grade, I wanted that convenience too. To that end, one year my big Christmas present was a portable two-burner propane stove. Unfortunately, I was never able to use it on a Scout campout though. Shortly after receiving it, we relocated to Florida and my next Scoutmaster was very, very traditional and wanted *all* meals cooked over an open fire.

If you have the time and capacity to cook a meal over an open fire, it is a neat experience (only every so often, though). But if you are trying to feed your hungry crew, the amount of time it takes to prepare the fire and do the cooking can cause more stress than it is worth. So cut yourself some slack and buy a nice two-burner propane stove. My preference is to buy a stove, and then use a griddle to grill things versus buying a road trip grill, and then trying to use pots on it. My suggestion is to focus on your stove being a stove versus being a grill. In case you are not familiar with the difference, a stove has a burner with a stove grate (for use with pots), while a grill has a burner with a grill grate (to cook food directly on it). Think Camp Chef Explorer versus Coleman Road Trip. While road trip grills are versatile, they tend to be better suited to tailgating where there is almost always grilling being done.

Coffee via a percolator can be ready in 10 minutes from flame to cup on a propane stove. Over an open fire, this might take 45 minutes. The same goes for hamburgers. Hamburgers can be ready in 10-15 minutes when using propane. When cooking over an open fire, it could take 45 minutes when you take into account the time it takes to get the coals ready.

Also, back to the subject of food being a mood changer . . . Burnt food that is full of ashes will *definitely* be a mood changer—a *bad* mood changer that is. Unless you know what you are doing, controlling the temperature of a wood-based fire requires some significant skill and experience. For this same reason, I recommend using charcoal briquettes for Dutch oven cooking versus wood. Different types of wood burn at different temperatures and can produce varying amounts of smoke and heat depending on the dryness of the wood.

A chuck box will make you the hero

In the Boy Scouts, each patrol (a group of 5-10 Scouts) has what they call a chuck box. A chuck box is usually a 3x2x2-foot wooden box that uses wooden legs to position it at counter height. Usually, at least one of the sides is hinged and opens up to provide a work surface. Each time the Scouts camp, they put their chuck box on its legs, open it up, and have all of the kitchen cooking items they need. This often includes pots, pans, silverware, plates, glasses, can openers, and seasonings.

Due to space constraints, my family does not have a chuck box. But we have a Rubbermaid Action Packer box we use like a chuck box. It is, unfortunately, much less organized than a real chuck box due to its lack of dividers. We use it for the same purpose however—to store all of our camping cooking gear. Over the years, we have worked to add items to it and now our chuck box is very well stocked.

Whenever we camp with others, without fail, we will have at least one family ask to borrow something out of our chuck box. And it is usually the same few items—the can opener, measuring cups, and measuring spoons. Every time, we come across looking like heroes. Most of the items we bring, we do so because we have either forgotten them ourselves previously or we have seen others forget them.

Stocking a chuck box is a lot of fun. Whenever we buy new items for our kitchen at home, we down-cycle any of the usable items to our chuck box. Yes, things are not in perfect cosmetic shape, but if they are functional, then we put them in our chuck box. This can lead to having four sets of measuring cups, though—so we have to occasionally purge our chuck box and pick out the best items. For our extras, we donate them to a Boy Scout troop in our area for use in their chuck boxes.

The items that should be in your chuck box that will make you seem like a superstar are measuring cups, measuring spoons, ladles, salt shaker, pepper grinder, lots of nice sharp knives, cutting boards, a collapsible colander, collapsible bowls, a grill brush, and a wire whisk.

Do not underestimate the importance of ample work surfaces

A cramped and unsanitary meal prep area can surely be frustrating. The solution is to have ample work surfaces to prepare your meals. Even if you and your crew eat all of your meals standing up, sitting on the ground, or sitting in camp chairs, you will still need an area to prepare your meals. Unfortunately, this is something that first-time or inexperienced campers tend to not think about until they realize they do not have enough meal prep space.

Here are some reasons you will want to have lots of food prep space: (1) need room to set items down, (2) need to keep raw foods separated from other foods—this is troublesome to do in a cramped space, (3) need a place to put hot items, (4) need a place that people can serve the food from, and (5) need a "coffee bar" area to add cream and sugar to your coffee.

While some campsites might have a picnic table, do not count on it. The easiest way to address having a sufficient amount of work surfaces is to purchase and bring your own folding 5-foot or 6-foot fold-in-half collapsible table. Within the past several years, the number and variety of tailgate tables has grown significantly. Please note that because these fold-in-half tables are often not as rugged as a one-piece collapsible table, you will need to be mindful of placing heavy items on top of them when traveling to and from the campsite. Whenever possible, I try to stand mine up vertically in the back of my SUV, and then pack items up against it to keep it upright. Unfortunately, one time I placed my Camp Chef stove and propane tank on top of it and ever since, the center now slightly slopes in.

Another option is to bring a vinyl tablecloth with the associated metal clips such as the checkerboard ones you often see. While you will most likely need or want this space for people to sit and eat, this will provide an extra work surface to prep your meals. I never plan on having a picnic table and just use them as bonus space when they are there.

Folding briefcase-style kitchens are an option as well. We have one that closes up into the space of a double-long briefcase. When unfolded, it provides a nice work surface. When we are tight on space in our vehicle, I will often bring my briefcase kitchen since it takes up such a small footprint in my car.

If there is not a picnic table at the campsite and you didn't bring a dedicated work surface, you will most likely end up preparing everything on the lid of your ice chest. Believe me—you do *not* want to do this for an entire weekend. It will be a very backbreaking experience. With that said, we have successfully used the top of an ice chest for making sandwiches on picnics. In fact, they now make some nice coolers that are well suited for this. I have even seen one that has a fold-out panel that converts the cooler into a small table.

Another desirable item to bring is an end table that can be placed beside and in-between your camping chairs. There are two styles that I like. One is the same style as the typical camping chair, but it has multiple side straps that are used to make the surface taut. The second style has aluminum planks that are strapped together. This metal variety has an impressive flat and hard surface but tends to be top-heavy and can topple over easily if bumped into by someone.

The end tables I do not like are the ones that are decorated as a checkerboard for playing checkers. These are absolutely insanely useless due to how loose and flimsy the surface is (since they tend to not have side straps). Unless your surface is completely taut, the checkers are going to slide down toward the center. What type of fun is that?

Start the day off right with breakfast

Your mother probably told you to not skip breakfast since it was the most important meal of the day. While there is some disagreement about this in today's times, I believe it absolutely still holds true on campouts. Timely and hot food for breakfast can positively impact everyone's mood and set the tone for the day.

Most important is the timeliness. If you have coffee drinkers, having hot coffee ready to go needs to be addressed first. With today's automatic timer-based coffeemakers, your barely awake and previously asleep campers are going to expect a cup of coffee first thing in the morning. While the first person to awake on the campout (which will most likely be you) will have to suffer for a bit until the coffee is ready, the goal is for everyone else to wake up to hot coffee. Also, since many people do not drink their coffee black, make sure to have a reasonable coffee bar

ready for them with a variety of creamers, sugars, and flavored syrups (like vanilla). You do not want your campers trying to learn (or re-learn) to drink black coffee on a campout—that would not be a wise thing to try. You can help speed things along by getting your coffeepot ready the night before with water, a paper filter, and coffee grounds. If you decide to go this direction, you will need to find a place to secure your coffeepot so that animals and bugs cannot get into it. I have had trouble with raccoons being attracted to the unused coffee grounds and clawing into my container of them. Since we typically camp within a few feet of our car, I will place the ready-to-go coffee pot on the floorboard of the car to prevent animals (and bugs) from getting into it.

Now, on to food. I would suggest bringing and eating a lot of fresh fruit for breakfast. Fresh fruit is something that just seems to pair itself with camping. I will often cut up strawberries and cantaloupe and place it in a bowl with blueberries and other high-antioxidant (bright bold color) fruits. Not only does this provide a balance to whatever breakfast you fix, it also allows your hungry crew to immediately have something to eat that is healthy too.

Regarding the main breakfast course, I prefer eggs and bacon, but I have found that most kids want pancakes and bacon. While not what we would do at home, I have found the best way to serve breakfast on a campout is to serve people directly from the griddle. We usually cook up the bacon, and as the pancakes (and/or eggs) become available, I go ahead and serve a member of my family who is standing patiently waiting with a plate in-hand. By doing this, my campers are able to eat while the food is still hot.

Lunches should be convenient

Somehow, lunchtime seems to sneak up on us on campouts. This can especially be true if breakfast KP didn't finish up until 9 a.m. Usually, I have found that a lunchtime where the prep starts at 11:30 a.m. and you eat between 11:45 a.m. to 12 p.m. works the best. Otherwise, your kids will be hounding you for a snack. And, if you give in to them, it will either delay lunch or leave a significant amount of lunch food uneaten.

The goal for lunch is for it to be convenient and not near the ordeal that breakfast might have been. Our family usually has sandwiches—either ham/turkey sandwiches or peanut butter and jelly. We have one child in our family who loves marshmallow crème, so we always bring it as a surprise for him. I guess since we bring it every time, it is not legitimately a surprise and is now just expected at this point. Regardless, we are always looking for ways to let our kids know how special they are, and if the small act of bringing a jar of marshmallow crème can do that, then fantastic.

As far as sandwich fixings, we usually wash and separate lettuce, cut tomatoes, and lay out the items for everyone. We also bring multiple bags of potato chips in some of the varieties that the kids love but are probably not the best for them—think Cheetos, Doritos,

and Funyuns. I know what you are thinking—didn't I say elsewhere to bring *healthy* food? While that is true, it is also nice to spoil your family with at least something they love that might lack a lot of nutritional value. Another special treat could be your lunchtime drink. If you are going to allow your kids to have a drink other than water, lunch is an opportune time to allow them to have a glass of lemonade or soda. I would suggest individual soda cans versus a 2-liter bottle so that when it is gone, it is gone. Also, because of the ease of this meal, pretty much any of your kids can help prepare and clean it up. Also, the only dirty dishes should be a few plates, knives, and forks. I say this because we usually just eat lunch on a paper towel so that we do not have to be bothered with cleaning plates afterward. Obviously, this does not work with little kids or when you put an item like fresh cut fruit on your plate. Because only a few things need to be cleaned, we usually do not set up a full cleanup system with the three tubs (to be discussed later in this book) at lunch. Instead, we just wash the items by hand with room temperature water and some dish soap. Usually, at campgrounds, the water spigot is attached to a wooden post right there at your campsite. We typically put a bottle of environmentally friendly dish soap on top of that flat-topped post for people to wash their hands or for these small cleanup jobs.

It is imperative to remember what lunch is supposed to be. It is not meant to be a midday feast but just a necessary meal at midday to refuel your body and to allow you to possibly catch your breath in preparation for more activities. Also, lunchtime (and campouts) is probably not the best time to convert picky eaters. If you have a kid who will only eat sandwiches with crunchy peanut butter, then do not try to switch to creamy on the campout. Try your best to make lunch a non-event. Some of my favorite campout moments have been sitting around in the shade at lunch and just chilling. Unlike breakfast and dinner, lunch should definitely be a relaxed meal.

Hot meals are always a fantastic option for lunch, and for various reasons, tend to be out of the norm on campouts. Typical options include hot dogs, hamburgers, and grilled cheese sandwiches—which are all fairly easy to prepare. Another option is Frito pie. This is where you mix chili (and other ingredients) with Frito brand corn chips in a Frito bag and eat the mixture right out of the bag. The first time I had this was at the 1982 Knoxville World's Fair when I was there with my high school marching band. Unfortunately, the one-ounce individual bags you get in a multipack Frito box today are just too small. Instead, you need the ones you find at the grocery store checkout lane or at a convenience store.

Here is how you make it. Heat the chili (mild with no beans) in a pot. Cut the sealed top of the Fritos bags off (one bag per person), add a scoop of chili, top with some shredded cheese, stir, and eat. Some simple variations include chopped onions, lettuce, tomatoes, and sour cream. Because we always use mild chili, I usually bring along a bottle of non-refrigerated hot sauce for those (like myself) that prefer something stronger than mild chili.

The noteworthy thing about Frito pie is that it provides a warm meal and the only individual utensil that gets dirty is your spoon (or fork). Since you eat directly out of the bag, there are no plates or bowls to cleanup. And you can just wait until you clean the dinner time dishes to clean what was dirtied at lunch.

Make the Saturday night dinner a feast

With a little bit of work, you can turn your dinner into a feast and impress your family. Let me give you examples of what I am talking about. Most of the time, Saturday night dinner on a campout means burgers and potato chips. If you stick with burgers, what are some things you can do to make your burger meal a feast? How about bringing some homemade potato salad? How about making some awesomely delicious BBQ baked beans? Sauté mushrooms and onions for the burgers? How about cooking fresh bacon or providing freshly sliced avocado? Here is an over-the-top one—cook up some fries in a skillet with hot grease or in a pot of oil. Think about what types of extras you are offered at the high-end burger places. You could even make some gourmet hamburger patties with various seasonings and blends of meat. If you are a hunter, offer a blend of beef or venison. How about some bison?

You could also cook something that your campers would only expect to have at home. How about a roast in a Dutch oven? How about shepherd's pie? Or how about fresh fajitas with freshly made guacamole that you make on-site? Maybe even make fresh salsa. Take a basic meal and just figure out how to add some zing to it. Also, you could consider making something 100 percent from scratch such as corn bread or state fair biscuits.

Also, plan to have a killer Dutch oven-based dessert right after the meal. And do not try to keep it a secret—the fact that a scrumptious dessert is coming can honestly help the dinner seem even better.

Using specialized outdoor cooking gear often leads to great memories

Whenever people experience something new, they tend to share the experience with others. I have seen this whenever people use a neat outdoor cooking gadget. So, if you have neat outdoor kitchen gadgets, bring them and train others to use them. Let them make it their memory—you already have yours from when you previously used it.

A case in point . . . I have an exceptional and easy-to-use device called a

CanCooker. It is essentially an expensive camping steamer. While they are on the shelves of the big box camping retailers, most people just walk on past them. They do not know what it is or what it does. Whenever we use ours, people are fascinated by how awesome the food turns out, how many people we can feed, and just how unique of a device it is. Part of the coolness comes from me telling everyone about the backstory related to the item. And since most people will not rush out to buy their own, they will definitely want to talk about what they do have—their memorable experience of using yours. Here are other some specialized outdoor cooking devices that people are amazed by (when coupled with my stories about why they are so cool):

- ☀ Egg Shaker with wire whisk beater ball
- ☀ Toaster – Coleman 4-piece
- ☀ Chain mail to clean cast iron
- ☀ Coffee Press
- ☀ Deep Fat Fryer – Coleman RoadTrip
- ☀ Pizza Oven
- ☀ Sun Cooker
- ☀ Box Cooker

Let me talk a little more about the CanCooker. As I have been told, the story behind it is that the creator grew up on his family's farm. Every morning, the farm workers would arrive with whatever they could contribute to a communal lunch and would drop it into a modified metal milk

jug. They would bring potatoes, corn, or other vegetables. The farm's owners would then throw in enough chicken for everyone as well. Sometime before lunch, someone would close up the cooker, add liquid and seasoning, and put it over an appropriate heat source. Forty-five minutes later, it would be ready and there would be enough steamed food to feed 15 people. I think that part of the neatness of the CanCooker is the communal aspect. The other is that once the steam plume is the correct height, you can sit and read a book or have a conversation with a friend while you watch the steam plume. Whenever we use ours, we place the optional wire rack in the bottom, and then place the food that needs to be cooked the longest on the bottom. We put half ears of corn on the bottom. You can fit at least 12 when you stand them up on end. First, however, before we put in any food, we coat the interior surfaces with butter cooking spray or rub the end of a stick of butter everywhere on the interior. We then put in the cut potatoes, baby carrots, mushrooms, baby onions, more butter, and a whole bottle of Italian salad dressing and one cup of water. Make sure you have some appetizing bread, butter, and honey to go with it. Also, since presentation is very key, just as we are about to eat, I pour the entire contents into a disposable aluminum roaster pan (the size intended for a 20 lb turkey). Doing so showcases this meal.

KP, mess kits, and why you should care

While many details are provided in the "Conservation Minded" chapter on the subject of KP, I wanted to provide a brief introduction here. First, I need to explain two key terms—*mess kits* and *KP*. Both have military foundations. Originally, a mess kit was a collection of silverware and cookware that could

double as a soldier's plate, bowl, and cup. Mess kits were typically made of lightweight aluminum so they could be used over an open flame as cookware and nested together into a compact footprint. In the context of modern camping, however, a mess kit is simply the silverware, plate, bowl, and cup you take camping. They are typically made of plastic and are

often BPA-free. Many will also come with a mesh drip bag. For those that want to be ultra-compact, you can purchase collapsible bowls that can also be used as a plate, and silverware where the spoon, fork, and knife are all one single utensil. For the most part, today's mess kits are not intended to be used as cookware. But for our discussions related to family camping, a mess kit is simply the reusable tableware you bring on a campout. It could even be unbreakable kids' plates from your kitchen cupboard you grab as you head out the door as you leave for the campout.

Now, on to KP. I use the term as meaning Kitchen Patrol, although I have also heard it referred to as Kitchen Police. As a military term, it actually had dual meanings. It could either mean the actual workers that assisted the military kitchen staff or could mean the work that was done under the direction of the kitchen staff. You have probably already been exposed to KP and didn't even know it. Think of all of those black-and-white war movies with the soldiers peeling potatoes while on KP as part of some disciplinary action. As it relates to family camping, the term KP today is commonly used to describe the act of cleaning up after a meal—not the food prep or cooking and not the people doing the work.

As I mention elsewhere in this book, things are just different on a campout. Some things are better than at home, and other things are not. For our family, cleaning up after a campout meal is one of those tasks that always works out much better than someone would expect. At home, parents tend to struggle with getting their kids to help clean up after a meal. But with the KP setup we use, my kids admittedly enjoy it, and I very rarely have trouble keeping everyone engaged. Because of the assembly line approach I use, up to 12 people can be working at the KP station. Also, because of the extra-large washtubs we use, we can have a two-sided KP line. Both kids and parents honestly seem to enjoy being able to talk to each other and bonding during KP. And I am not kidding. Whenever we camp with others, we often see the kids from those families abandon their own family's cleanup responsibilities to come help with ours. Because our KP setup can handle so many people, I will also open our setup to others to use as well. It provides a way to get to know other people. Our guests unquestionably enjoy learning about the KP process, seeing their kids help (which is sometimes a first), and also getting their dishes clean. So, definitely leave those paper plates at home and start looking forward to KP.

Having the right cooler and using it correctly is important to your health

Recently, I helped a young man as the counselor on a cooking-related badge. Many of the initial requirements were all related to safety. Although I knew most of the information, it was extremely helpful to go through it again. While the biggest safety issues in the home kitchen are related to cuts and burns, on campouts there are additional concerns. An area that truly concerns me is food-borne issues due to a lack of sanitation and a lack of proper refrigeration.

Several years ago, I was camping with a group of adult men and found out that the man who was in charge of the Saturday breakfast had only put a couple of cold ice packs in his huge almost empty cooler. Inside the cooler was our sole supply of eggs, milk, and other items that needed to be stored cold. When I asked him if he wanted me to add some ice, I found out that he honestly had no reservations at all about our food being at essentially room temperature. At least with burns, you know immediately if you got hurt. With food-borne issues due to improper refrigeration, you do not find out until later in many cases.

Another lesser area of concern is associated with diseases from wild animals that come in contact with your food (if they break into your ice chest or dry goods box). Making sure to secure your food from animals is a must-do on campouts. And if animals do come in contact with your food, I would suggest not eating anything that was not completely shielded (via a metal can or other hard container). If your ice chest does not have raccoon-proof latches, then you need to use another mechanism such as a ratcheting-style packing strap. You can use a bungee cord, but there is a real problem with them. While they will keep the raccoons out, the raccoons may play with it trying to get it off by stretching it out, and then letting it go. And they may do so all night. If you do not mind hearing a loud *"pop"* all night as the bungee cord slaps down on the top of the cooler, then go right ahead and use a bungee cord to keep your cooler shut.

Now, on to my biggest concern—keeping food cold on a campout.

Let's think about how a cooler works. First, it does not "cool" items. Instead, it helps to maintain items at the temperature they were put in at. This is done primarily via insulation. Most coolers have some form of insulation that prevents the cold from the food from being transferred out of the cooler. Second, it allows your cooling agent (usually ice) to cool your food and not your cooler. The better quality cooler you have (from an insulation perspective), the less cooling agent you will need.

While I have purposely avoided naming specific brands in this book, I have made a few exceptions. One of these exceptions is regarding one of the best brands of coolers out there today which is YETI. Here is some information behind the science of a YETI cooler. When shopping for a cooler, look for these qualities in other coolers as well. The following came directly from the YETI.com website.

"So what's the big deal and just what makes a Yeti cooler so strong? It all starts with the manufacturing process of the shell itself. Just like your kayak, YETI coolers are roto-molded rendering a product that has no seams..."

"While durability has sky-rocketed YETI to fame, it's the ability to do what coolers are meant to do that has pushed these products into the limelight—keeping your food and drinks cold and fresh. YETI coolers use up to 3 inches of pressure-injected commercial grade polyurethane foam in the walls and lid to make sure your ice stays ice all day long. Let's just say if your ice isn't cold, your ice is broken, not your YETI."

Regardless of what brand or style of cooler you have, the following tips will help you to use your cooler to its fullest potential. Just like my comments about knowing how to properly clean your dishes, knowing how to keep your food cool on a campout is critically important.

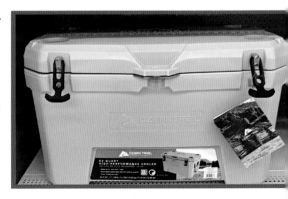

If your cooler is warm when you get ready to use it (most likely from being stored in a warm place like your attic or garage), a significant amount of ice will be wasted cooling the cooler itself. Therefore, relocate your cooler to a climate-controlled space the day before you plan on using it. Then, a few hours prior to use, pre-cool it with a sacrificial bag of ice. Assuming this bag of ice did not melt too much, you could potentially refreeze it and use it to precool your ice chest again in the future.

It should be noted that ice which is colder than the freezing point of 32 degrees is fairly dry and will last significantly longer. Therefore, if you can, attempt not to add melting ice to your cooler since it will most likely only be at 32 degrees.

The way that heat (or cold distribution) works is that everything that is cooler will try to reach the same temperature. This includes air inside your cooler. The cooling agent will try to cool it too. Therefore, large areas of air inside your cooler will quickly consume the cold from the cooling agent. If using ice, this means the ice will melt faster. If you are not able to use the correct-sized cooler, then fill this dead space with extra ice or towels. You can even use newspaper that has been crumpled up.

Once your cooler is in use, do not empty the cold water since it will almost be as cold as the ice and will help insulate the remaining ice. However, food that needs to be refrigerated (including meat) should be kept out of the water.

Every time you open the cooler, you are exchanging the cold air inside for warm air outside that must then be now cooled, causing the ice to melt faster. If you can find a cooler with a quick small access panel for grabbing a single bottle of water or soda, that would be preferable. That is, as long as this access panel has an adequate seal or gasket.

If your cooler is not the best, I suggest freezing any foods you will use for the second evening's dinner. For example, when we make Dutch oven shepherd's pie, we freeze the cooked meat/onion mixture and the shredded cheese. We also use frozen vegetables instead of canned ones. From the time we leave our home on Friday afternoon until Saturday night, these items are acting like giant ice cubes for everything else in the cooler. If you do have a high-performance cooler, you might need to pull these items out early if they are supposed to be cooked at or near room temperature on Saturday night.

Also, remember that if you have one of those top-of-the-line coolers, you need to secure it with a cable to a tree or a similar permanent object. In fact, many of them now come with built-in places to run a cable lock. While you might think you are being smart to put your high-end cooler in the back of your SUV, people have been known to break into a car to get one of these high-end and high-dollar coolers. Most campers are upstanding, but unfortunately, not all of them.

Use a dry box the right way
so you do not end up feeding the raccoons

Hungry critters will quickly trash your food supply if not properly stored. While we have already discussed securing your refrigerated/frozen items in your cooler via a packing strap, we now need to discuss doing the same for your dry goods. Dry goods are all of the foods and seasonings that do not need to be refrigerated (or at least do not need to be refrigerated until they have been opened). Animals have a keen sense of smell and can detect odors right through boxes of cereal and bags of potato chips. If it is food, then it needs to be secured. Not just at night but during the day as well. Especially, if you are going to be away from your campsite very long. Animals in state parks are smart and seriously do watch you from the woods—waiting for you to leave. Do not let this overly concern you, however. For the most part, the animals are not interested in you at all—just the food that you brought. Note that animals (especially the nocturnal ones) do like to get into food more so at night, though.

The easiest solution and lowest cost one is to put your dry goods back in your car when not being used. When we are able to park right next to our campsite, this is what we typically do. We open the back hatch on our SUV and have our own little pantry right there ready to go.

A better longer-term option is to purchase a dry goods box. Since offerings are always changing, I would suggest getting input from others about what has worked for them and has not gotten broken into by animals. You can additionally look at the posts on TheKeenCamper.com website as well for my current recommendations. Presently, I like the 24-gallon Action Packer by Rubbermaid. Rubbermaid used to make three sizes but now only make two, and as you can guess, the size that was discontinued (which I believe was a 12-gallon one) was the best suited for dry goods.

Here are items that I would place in a dry goods box:

- Potato chips
- Boxed cereal
- Granola bars—even individually wrapped ones
- Cookies
- Lemonade mix
- Coffee beans and grinds
- Seasonings
- Bread
- Unopened condiments—ketchup, mustard, and mayo
- Any food that does not need to be refrigerated
- Canned foods
- Vegetables & fruits that do not need to be refrigerated—like potatoes and onions

A few years ago, I took a group of fourth-grade and fifth-grade boys (and their parents) to a half-week summer camp. While we were not responsible for preparing our own meals, we still generated a fair amount of trash at our campsite. Because our campsite was somewhat remote from the rest of the camp, each night we would take our trash bag and tie it up from the rafters of the pavilion at our campsite. Each morning, we would untie it and place it back on the ground at the side of the pavilion. Why we believed at that time that raccoons were only hungry at night and would thus only be mischievous at night is beside me.

After we took the trash bag down each morning, we would typically leave for breakfast and not return until after lunch. One day we returned to find our trash bag ripped to shreds and our trash strewn everywhere. It turns out those raccoons were in the woods surrounding out campsite just waiting for us to leave so that they could strike. While I have not experienced it, I have heard of others having the same issue with animals getting into lunch-related food left out on a picnic table. Also, due to potential health issues, if the food does come into contact with animals (via their mouths or paws), trash it. If a bag of chips or a loaf of bread has been ripped open by a raccoon, immediately dispose of it too. Hopefully, by now, you are convinced of the importance of bringing and using a dry goods box.

Break out of the norm and have healthy drinks and snacks

Have you ever been on a car trip and after a while you just felt kind of gross? Not so much from the recirculated air and the general travel grunge but because of all of the junk food you have been eating—sodas, candy, potato chips, and packaged cookies. Now, think about how you would feel on those trips if you were snacking on fresh fruit, vegetables, homemade bread, and only drinking water. Kind of a better experience—right?

Well, I suggest trying the same thing on a campout—especially regarding what you drink. I suggest keeping it to water. But if you are expecting your

crew to only drink water, please bless them with filtered (and possibly bottled) water. I would also suggest having a separate and dedicated ice chest just for your drinks. This will save you a lot of stress and will keep your refrigerated food items safe until they are needed. This way, if the drink cooler keeps on getting opened (especially since kids like to play with the ice), it will not impact the coldness of your food. And, you will not have to be constantly getting on to your kids for leaving the cooler lid open.

For snacks, I suggest the same thing. We usually buy a large bag of oranges or tangerines. I enjoy having oranges on campouts and peeling them with my pocketknife. This is something I started doing at a summer camp years ago, and it has been a tradition ever since. In the morning, I put an orange in my day pack for midmorning when I get hungry. Fresh cut vegetables and fresh bread (such as banana bread) from home are options as well. Ditch all of the junk food—chips, candy, and store-bought cookies. Since I am partial to oatmeal cookies, sometimes we will bake a batch at home to bring with us. Years ago, I attended a training campout and another leader brought a batch of oatmeal cookies. They were, hands-down, the best oatmeal cookies I have ever had. Now, bringing them on a campout has become a tradition and ties back to a pleasant camping memory from years before. Please note that while you might eat a significant number of them on the campout, they are super healthy.

Here are items to consider bringing:

- Apples
- Halos, Cuties, oranges
- Fresh cut vegetables
- Almond butter (especially flavored almond butter) with disposable spoons
- Celery
- Homemade cookies
- Homemade banana bread
- Nuts such as walnuts and almonds

Take the lead, involve the kids, and give your spouse a break

While everyone's family dynamics are different, I am going to assume that most of the meal prep work falls to one of the parents and that the children do not help very much. Assuming that you are the one that does not help that much with meals, I would like to suggest that you give your spouse or partner a break. And do not just take on the work yourself. Instead, involve your kids as well. It will provide a time to fellowship with your family and could be a very empowering experience for your kids. With most campout meals, there is something that everyone can do.

One of my favorite meals for building a strong family relationship is chili. Let me give you an example. Here is the work that will need to be done:

- ☀ Cut and dice onions
- ☀ Break garlic bulbs into cloves
- ☀ Peel garlic cloves
- ☀ Mince garlic
- ☀ Open cans of beans
- ☀ Pour cans of beans into the pot
- ☀ Open cans of diced tomatoes
- ☀ Pour cans of diced tomatoes into the pot
- ☀ Cook hamburger meat
- ☀ Stir the chili

Here is how I have involved most of my kids when we make chili. I will let my 5-year-old hold the cans while my 8-year-old opens them. The 5-year-old then pours the contents into the pot. My 15-year-old and 13-year-old cut onions while my 10-year-old cooks the hamburger meat.

And while there are a lot of specialized tools to cut onions and to prepare the garlic, we do both with fairly old-school methods so that we can spend more time together cooking. We often use a lot of terrific Pampered Chef brand tools too—especially the ones for garlic since they have safety designed into them, which is critical when letting kids do things. For example, The Pampered Chef can opener opens the cans from the side leaving them virtually free of sharp edges.

My first experience with this recipe and getting lots of kids involved was when I took a group of fourth-graders camping and wanted us to all work on dinner together. Before this, the boys had always relied on the parents to cook the meals. But I needed a recipe where all of the boys could do something. There is a funny story about why we had so much work for the boys to do to make this chili recipe. I had been given the recipe by a friend and had never made it before. It called for three garlic cloves for a recipe that would feed 15 people. The person that bought the food did not read the recipe very carefully and bought three garlic bulbs. Not reading the recipe very closely myself and definitely not properly thinking through things, we ended up putting in all three garlic bulbs which was about 30 cloves. Believe it or not, the chili was amazing, and to this date, we continue to put one entire bulb (not three since that *really* was insane) into this chili recipe. This recipe was great primarily because it gave the boys so much to do. It allowed the boys to stand around my fold-up briefcase-kitchen talking for over an hour while they prepared the cloves. And because the amount of garlic skin that fell to the ground during the process was crazy, they had even more work to do together to clean it all up afterward.

Another way to keep everyone busy is to have some kids start working on the dessert. As covered in the Dutch Ovens chapter in the second volume of *The Keen Camper Camping with Kids* book series, making dump cake cobblers is super easy and involves prep work that all ages can do. The only part that indeed needs to be done perfectly is the process of lining the Dutch oven with foil, which will require a little bit of parental coaching.

So, give the normal cook in your family a break. Let that person sit and read or lie in a hammock. You could also suggest that person take a walk or go sit down by the lake to have some actual "me" time while you and your kids work on the dinner. And other people's kids will often ask to help as well. Definitely, let them since their parents might not have planned something like this. Just remember to invite them (and their parents) over for a bowl of chili or a scoop of dessert later. To that end, we also make hefty meals on campouts so that nobody goes hungry and so that we can share it with others. I have been known to walk around after our meal with a Dutch oven in each hand offering those who did not make an awesome dinner or dessert some leftovers.

Having a getaway breakfast will help your last morning to be less stressful

Unfortunately, many of us are undoubtedly overscheduled, and because of that on Sunday morning (the last day of most campouts), we are not thinking about chilling. Instead, we are thinking about getting going, the list of chores waiting for us at home, going to work the next day, and all of the unpacking. Also, some people want to get going due to the heat and sweatiness involved with packing up later in the day. While most of us arrive on Friday evening when it is somewhat cool, on late Sunday morning or midafternoon, the sun is at its highest, and it can be hot. If you are strong enough to get past all of the above challenges and can enjoy your last day on the campout, then you can ignore the following. If not, I have at least one idea that will help your Sunday morning to be a little less stressful.

My suggestion is to not cook on Sunday morning and to have what a friend of mine calls a "getaway breakfast." It is a breakfast that does not require any cooking. Also, you typically eat standing around your campsite before you start packing up. We like to get some outstanding gourmet bagels from Panera Bread or Einstein Brothers Bagels with a few tubs of flavored cream cheese on Friday afternoon before we head out to the campout. We usually keep the bagels in a cool place where they will not sweat or get hard. We also usually eat whatever fresh fruit is left over and sometimes even bring individual yogurts. While I said that our getaway breakfast does not require any cooking, we will occasionally heat water to mix with instant packs of oatmeal. That leaves us with only a few dirty knives, spoons, and cups (for juices, coffee, and oatmeal) to clean up before we leave.

The getaway breakfast has made a big difference to our family's stress level on Sunday morning. No more cleanup after pancakes, eggs, and bacon. No waiting for griddles to cool down before being packed up. And if we did have rain on Sunday morning, no trying to cook in that either. Also, we look forward to this breakfast because we have not allowed ourselves to eat any of these delicious bagels or yogurts until that Sunday morning.

When I have camped with a large number of people, I have used the getaway breakfast approach as well, but on a much-larger scale. I usually find a local donut place near the campground and go back into town before everyone gets up to get donuts. I did this for a group of nearly 100 people once. We had a plug-in-style 42-cup percolator coffee maker and enough donuts (glazed and chocolate iced) for everyone to have a few each. It was a huge hit with everyone. As a bonus, since nobody had to cook breakfast on Sunday morning, this allowed everyone to attend our church service without feeling rushed, hungry, or guilty for abandoning their KP responsibilities at their campsites. We also had bottles of various juices (including orange juice) for the kids. This group positively loved coffee. So much so that we ended up making three batches of coffee with that 42-cup percolator. To help the donut shop and its normal Sunday customers, I would suggest placing your order the day before so that you do not buy all of their donuts or cause other customers to have to wait for your order to be filled before they get theirs.

One final point to this section is that in many areas, both school-based camping trips and Cub Scout packs like to do 1-night camping trips with you arriving on Saturday and departing on Sunday. In these cases, if you do not cook on Sunday morning, your kids will miss the very memorable experience of a hot breakfast on a campout. In this situation, it is my recommendation to cook while you're there, or make it a 2-night campout with the cooked breakfast being done on Saturday morning.

Coffee and other hot drinks are critical

Just like with hot meals, there is something very soothing about a hot drink. And it does not have to be coffee. It can also be black tea, herbal teas, apple cider, or hot chocolate. I find tea to be the most calming though. As a family, both my wife and I are coffee drinkers and some of my kids are as well—yes, I know I am a bad parent for letting them develop a caffeine addiction at such an early age. While I like tea, I start my day off with a cup of coffee.

Let's take the day in stages. If you have morning coffee drinkers, definitely have coffee waiting for them when they wake up. The best option for a campout is to use a stove top percolator. Interestingly, most people these days have no idea what a coffee percolator is. One thing that I like about a percolator is that you can increase the strength of the batch by letting it circulate additional times. If you can, I would recommend buying a family size (28 quart) pot. You do not want to run out of coffee in the morning, and it is rewarding to be able to offer coffee to others who were not as prepared as you. Also, it is an easy way to meet people by inviting them over to your campsite for a cup of coffee. You can even bring your pot (and some disposable lidded cups) to their campsites as well.

We also bring a truly unique tea infuser from Teavana and an assortment of flavored caffeinated and decaffeinated teas. Unlike traditional black tea (or coffee), these teas are very easy on your stomach. The only downside is our tea infuser is a single-serving style. And who wants to drink by themselves? Therefore, you might want to buy a second one or a larger double one. A neat feature of this infuser is that it sits on top of your mug and drains right into it after the steeping. Having two single infusers will allow each person to brew a different cup of tea. I also like that both this tea infuser and our coffee percolator feel very "earthy" and somewhat old school while at the same time being well designed and engineered. As usual, take a look at TheKeenCamper.com website for my present recommendations.

And for your kiddos that are not coffee or tea drinkers, have hot chocolate and hot apple cider available for them on those cold mornings and evenings. You can buy them in individual packets and add either warm water or milk to them.

Another neat gadget I have heard of is a manual Keurig where you insert a K-cup, and then pour hot water through it. That might be an easy way to do hot chocolate on a campout as well. The only downside is the relatively high price of each K-cup. But since the point of a campout is to have a great time, it is probably an expense that is well worth it due to the ease of preparing hot chocolate this way.

What lessons in leading your family can you take away from this aspect of camping?

"Orchestration and Conducting"

Orchestration and conducting are the two words I want you to take away from this chapter. Yes, this chapter is officially about Food & Cooking, but it is in fact about something much more fundamental. Assuming that you agree with me that one of the primary purposes for a family is teaching, then this section will hopefully be very relevant. As most parents have experienced, "talking to" someone is probably one of the least effective ways to teach someone. Think about your own life—how often did you learn something (undeniably learned something) when your parents made comments like *"you need to start taking better care of your things"* or *"you need to spend more time studying"*? As an adult, how receptive are you when your boss barks *"you need to produce more results"* or *"you need to produce higher quality work"*? The best teachers are those that take the time to put together experiences that will teach versus ineffective words.

For campouts, my goal is for my family to look forward to the meals, to be excited about preparing them, and to want to engage with others to do this work together. Telling my family *"you need to fix dinner while working together and you better not complain afterward"* is just not going to cut it.

Instead, I work behind the scenes to create circumstances where they can work right alongside each other performing meaningful tasks at their level. And by doing this repeatedly over a number of outings, many of my older children are now able to cook independently on their own now. Yes, I could have cooked all of the meals and that would have been a huge blessing to my family, but the blessing of teaching them a skill was much more valuable.

Recently, I took my oldest son and a group of his friends and their fathers on a sailing trip in the Bahamas. It was an experience of a lifetime. While the Bahamas were amazing, the best memory was the 13 of us working together. This included running the boat and cooking all of our own meals. Ahead of time, the captain had orchestrated things well. He had a nice galley (kitchen), plenty of working space, an outdoor gas grill, lots of pots and pans, and a variety of high-quality food (including steaks and pork chops). Several of the adults who happened to be excellent cooks worked with the boys on each cooking shift regarding ideas on how they could use the available food to put together some amazing meals since there was not a menu.

On the other hand, I have a friend that a week later took his family on a similar sailing ship that had a crew of three instead of just a captain. They also had an unbelievable time, but all of their meals were prepared for them. While their trip definitely met their need to relax and to get reinvigorated for the rest of their summer, mine met my goal—to teach the boys how to work together to run a ship, to enjoy doing so, and to achieve superior results.

Another relevant example is one I heard in a Love & Logic parenting class. They told about a parent who wrote in about how she decided to deal with a child that was continually throwing fits on their shopping trips. The child would act out and when the mother would say they were going to leave, the child would refuse to leave. The mother would eventually cave and give into the child's demands. After much frustration, the mother arranged with a friend (that the child was very familiar with) to be at a specific retail store at a certain day and time. I believe they were coordinating via text the day of as well. When the usual situation arose and the child refused to leave, the mother told the child she was leaving, and then did. Within a few minutes, the other mother came up to the child and asked what was going on and offered to take the child back to the child's house. While I do not know if this story is true (and I'm not sure if this approach might get you in some trouble with the police and the department store), it demonstrates someone taking the initiative to both orchestrate and then conduct a teaching moment that I am sure the child would never forget.

I challenge you to think about what things you want to teach your kids, and how you can best do so in a manner that is very organic and natural. Yes, this is going to challenge you to do more than just call your kids over and say, "*Hey, kids, I want to tell you something*" or "*Hey, kids, I want to show you something*." I would argue that the value of one thoroughly orchestrated and conducted teaching opportunity is more valuable than 50 ones that are primarily verbal or with limited interaction.

So, as I close this chapter, think about the following: What is orchestration and what is conducting? According to *Webster's Dictionary*, "orchestration" is *"to arrange or manipulate, especially by means of clever or thorough planning or maneuvering"* and "conducting" is *"to lead or guide"* or *"to direct (an orchestra, chorus, etc.) as leader."* If you are like me, your default teaching style probably does not including either conducting or orchestration. With that said, make a decision today to take a different approach for at least some (if not all) of your teaching and parenting going forward.

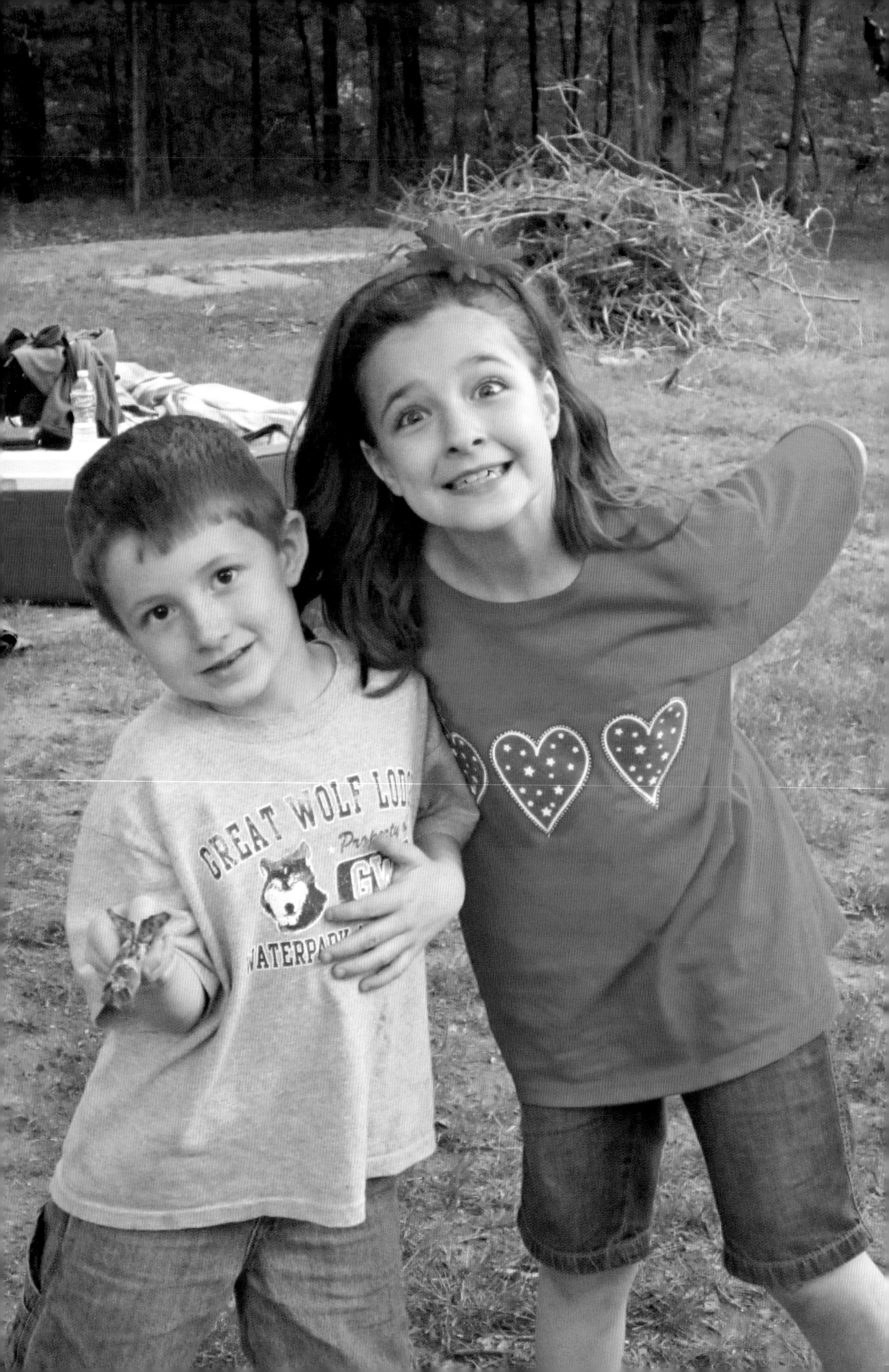
GREAT WOLF
WATERPARK

CHAPTER 3

TIMING

Being aware of timing can improve the success of your campout

Timing and awareness of timing can greatly improve the success of your campout. While the goal is for everyone to have a relaxing time, you as the leader will probably have to sacrifice a little bit so that your family can have the best experience. Being aware of timing does not mean looking at your watch every minute and micro-scheduling your campout. It just means being aware of the impact of how "when" you choose to do certain activities can create a domino effect on other activities. While you might have decided that you need to start a certain event by 4 p.m., your family does not have to know this. You can let them proceed on being totally carefree but know that when it gets to 4 p.m., you need to corral them and guide them on to something else. As a rule of thumb, choose some odd times like 4:07 p.m. so that it will be less obvious that you possibly have them on a schedule. It might be a good idea to bring your spouse onboard let them know that you have things under control and to trust you when you indicate it is time to move on to what is next.

While nobody likes to see others suffer, your family will quickly see how the flow of their campout is much smoother, more peaceful, and less chaotic than that of others you might be camping with (or see camping at the campground). I hope you will benefit from the lessons I have learned about timing and campout optimization. This goes along with a motto that I continue to share with my kids: "a smart person learns from their mistakes while a wise person learns from the mistakes of others." Please let the lessons I have learned from my mistakes help you to be wise regarding campout timing.

The fall is traditionally a great time to camp

Coffee mug in hand and sitting around a campfire with one of my little ones snuggled next to me—that is a moment to cherish. And for the most part, a campout memory you can only achieve during the fall camping season. Yes, you can camp throughout the entire year. In fact, my son's Boy Scout troop camps every single month—rain, shine, freezing temperatures, snow, and even 100-degree days. But for your family, you probably want to go a less die-hard route.

Camping in the fall has the following advantages:

- ☀ The weather tends to be more predictable in most regions of the country.
- ☀ The temperature tends to be milder— warm enough during the day to not wish you were inside and but yet cold enough at night that you will get a great night's sleep (using the methods I describe elsewhere in this book).
- ☀ There tends to be less rain.
- ☀ With so many kids having high school football games, band, and other fall sports, most state parks have more availability in the fall.
- ☀ You do not need to bring extreme weather equipment such as fans or heaters.
- ☀ Being around a campfire is actually enjoyable.

- ☀ It is not too hot to enjoy drinking a cup of coffee.
- ☀ You can snuggle with your kids around a campfire.
- ☀ It is easier to keep your food refrigerated since your ice is not constantly melting.
- ☀ There tends to be fewer bugs.
- ☀ In most places, the foliage is much prettier.

Camping in the spring does pose some challenges

Unpredictable as it might be, the spring provides one of the two most desirable time periods to take your family camping. While the fall is still my favorite recommendation due to more predictable temperatures, the spring has some nice offerings as well. First, after being cooped up all winter, people are usually eager and excited to get outside, and what better way to do that than a spring family camping trip. Camping in the spring does present some challenges that you need to be fully aware of, though. Thinking through these potential issues ahead of time can help you have the most optimal time.

The first issue is that there tends to be more rain in the spring. This is especially true for camping in April and moving on toward May—remember the saying, "April showers bring May flowers"? Having the right gear and attitude is critical in case you find yourself with rain throughout the trip. You would definitely want to have an instant-up style canopy too. Also, you might want to identify a list of nearby inside activities that you can do if it rains—preferably ones unique to the area such as restaurants and museums. Having spare clothes, shoes, and possibly even mud boots are all critical as well.

The following is one of my best experiences with family camping in the rain. I took a group of families on a campout where it rained from the time we set up our tents on Friday night through when we packed up on Sunday morning. The owner of this private ranch later told me she could not believe we stuck it out. But here were the keys. We had a large pavilion that we could gather under, cook beside, and eat under. We even had our "fireless" campfire under it. Also, since we did not have any lightning or hazardous weather, we allowed the kids to play outside in the rain. They got themselves completely filthy and wet multiple times each day. We even took a hayride in the rain with everyone wearing their raincoats. But after everything was said and done, it was one our best campouts ever.

A few years later, I took a group of boys and dads on a fishing-themed campout. It also rained the entire weekend. But we were able to rent a nearby covered pavilion which helped us a lot as well. When not fishing, the boys hung out under the pavilion, played cards, and did other things. We even had a fantastic fish fry where we cooked beside the pavilion and only minimally got wet. The key thing on both of these campouts was that we had some form of cover as part of a backup plan.

In the spring, it is always worth considering renting a pavilion near your campsite. If you are camping with a Scout unit or with multiple families, it can actually be reasonably priced if distributed across multiple people. When you compare this cost with all of the other money and time you have spent on the campout—the food you purchased, the campsite fees, the gas to the campground, the amount of work required to pack, and the amount that will be required afterward—the small cost of the pavilion is well worth it.

Another thing is to bring large black garbage bags. These can be used to put different parts of your tent in when packing up. We usually put the rainfly and the tent in one bag since they are wet but not very dirty and the tarp or ground cloth in another. If you pack your tent wet, once you get home—and I am specifically referring to the actual *day you get home*—you absolutely *need* to set up your tent in your garage or outside (if it is not raining). It should dry within a few hours. If you do not let your tent dry out, you could possibly end up having to throw it away due to mildew and mold issues. It does not take long for the mold smell to lock in permanently into your gear.

Another issue is the unpredictability of the temperature of the spring. It might be hot enough to wear shorts, but then again, it might not. It might be warm enough to swim (at least warm enough for the kids), but once again, it might not. It also might be cold enough for hot chocolate around the campfire, but possibly not. Therefore, you will need to bring a lot of extra gear "just in case."

Hot weather camping is best suited for those who truly love to camp

Sometimes I forget that the weather and climate are drastically different in different parts of our country. Here in Texas, summer is one of the more challenging times to camp comfortably, whereas, in Colorado, it might be the absolute best month. On the last day of a recent summer camp here in Texas, one of the other fathers shared some challenges he was having. He mentioned the additional gear that he needed to buy within the next few weeks. I was perplexed and thought that he was just super gung-ho about next year. It turns out he was planning on camping with his older son a few weeks later during the month of July here in Texas. He said they had moved from Kentucky, and did not have a need for mosquito nets, battery-operated fans, and car chargers to power the fans when camping there. After this subsequent campout with his older son, he said that the experience had been much better now that he had the appropriate gear.

So, should camping in the summer be relegated to only those that love camping? The answer is "it depends." It in fact depends on two things—where you live, and if this is truly the only time you and your family can possibly go on an extended weeklong campout.

Assuming that wherever you live, there are more bugs and it is hotter in the summer, then these are the two areas you need to plan for and mitigate against—heat and bugs. The concern about bugs is threefold:

- ☀ Bugs are annoying.
- ☀ Bugs are unsanitary.
- ☀ Bugs can lead to health issues.

During the day, there are things you can do when you find you are being swarmed by bugs. At night, you need some additional protection. If you are in a traditional tent, you need to keep it zipped up. If you are in an open-air tent (such as those 1950s Boy Scout summer camp-style ones) you will need a mosquito net. There are lots of other options to better control bugs such as installing screened sides on your instant-up canopy, using bug spray, burning citronella candles, and applying essential oils.

The issues with an increased temperature are threefold as well:

- ☀ It can leave you exhausted due to the extra calories your body is expending just keeping cool.
- ☀ You can feel uncomfortable due to the sweat.
- ☀ You can have an increased risk of heat stroke and heat exhaustion.

Do not take this last point too lightly. Recently, there was a case in the news regarding a European couple dying of heat-related issues at a national park in New Mexico within three hours of hitting the trail due to the heat and dehydration.

Cold weather camping is not just for people who like cold weather

In the winter, it is absolutely critical that you know the weather forecast. Unlike camping in hot weather, with cold weather camping, it is more painful to adjust "on the fly." If you wake up in the morning and do not have appropriate clothing, you will be miserable and might even get sick or have trouble from exposure. If you go to bed and you are freezing, you could also get sick or experience something even worse. These are situations where you cannot just magically produce a jacket, long pants, or a better sleeping bag.

So, regarding the winter, I do suggest that you make sure you know the weather report. Also, pay keen attention to the predicted morning lows. While a splendid day might be in the forecast, until those morning chills burn off, you might be uncomfortable for a few hours. The only time that I have been known to cancel a campout (or my attendance) is when it was predicted to be freezing during the days. Unless there is a compelling reason to be on this specific campout at this specific time, there is no reason to be out in the freezing elements barely surviving until the next meal and bedtime.

Also, remember that in the late fall and early spring, the weather can sometimes be positively unpredictable. Another thing to consider is where you are camping. We went to a summer camp in Colorado a few years back where it was short-pants weather in the day, in the 40s at night, and rained off and on. Once again, proper planning made a big difference. We wore clothes that could easily be layered and taken on and off as the temperature changed.

Arriving well before dark will reduce your setup stress

Pitch black outside with the moon being the only light source around is ideal for stargazing but not for putting up a tent and setting up your campsite. The first campout I went on with my family (and the first one in over 20 years for myself), we arrived at noon since it was a 1-day campout. I guess that gave me the false and mistaken sense of security that setting up a tent was not too involved. That was until our next campout the following spring when we arrived well after dark. The only light source I had was a propane lantern that was packed deep inside my vehicle and needed to have the propane tank located and screwed on as well. Fortunately, all of the other families that had arrived before dark were willing to help us get set up. I was very thankful for them and their kindness. A funny side note about this specific night . . . Later that night, we were finally in the tent and had been trying to go to sleep for a while when I just could not take it any longer. It was well past lights out. Who still had their lantern on? It was so bright and so close to our tent that we could not fall asleep. I angrily put on my shoes and stomped outside to see who I was going to need to confront. Well, what did I find? I found "my" lantern that I had set down when we set up the tent hours ago. Things were so crazy setting up our tent in the dark that I had forgotten about my lantern. It had been burning through my limited propane supply and had probably been keeping others awake for the past few hours at the same time. Fortunately, this unattended lantern did not fall over and catch my tent or the leaves on fire.

After camping with my son's Boy Scout troop for the past several years, I now have this setting-up-camp-in-the-dark thing down. I bring a headlamp and have it in an outside pocket of my day pack which is in the car with me, have my tent strategically located closest to my SUV's tailgate (so it is the first thing I take out), have a small backpacking tent that one person can easily put up in 5 to 10 minutes, and have plenty of lights with carabiners to hang from the canopy inside my tent.

But when I camp with my wife and kids, we try to arrive at least two hours before sunset. In the dark, you can easily lose kids and things you need to put the tent up (like the stakes and poles), it is hard to tell which way the rainfly goes, and it is tough to survey the campsite to find the best place for your tent (and to not place it in front of an anthill or next to a dead animal or under a tree branch that is just waiting to fall on your tent and your family). Picking the best location and orientation for your tent needs to happen in the daylight.

Once again, my suggestion is to plan to arrive at least two hours before sunset, and then to immediately get your tent setup and your personal gear put inside it. Then, assign someone to arrange the sleeping gear (my kids usually argue over who gets to do this since it does not require being outside anymore), and then everyone else helps to get

the campsite and cooking gear set up. Otherwise, when you and your crew wake up the following morning, you will then need to find and set up all of the gear to cook breakfast. Trust me, the next morning you will sincerely regret not having taken care of getting your kitchen area setup the night before—especially if you are wanting and desperately needing a cup of hot coffee first thing in the morning.

If you do end up arriving after dark, here are some recommendations that will help make the situation less stressful:

- ☀ Have the gear you need first conveniently packed for quick access
  - ☼ Tarp
  - ☼ Tent
  - ☼ Mallet
  - ☼ Tent lights
  - ☼ Lantern
  - ☼ Doormat

- ☀ Have a headlamp for everyone old enough to wear one.

- ☀ Have your headlamps in the car (and not packed up) so that they are available when you get out of the car. Make sure they all have fresh batteries.

- ☀ Put your little ones at a picnic table or leave them in the car with something to entertain them, or assign one of your older kids to watch them. Do not let them wander around in the dark. Providing them a snack will also assist with keeping them entertained.

- ☀ Crank on your propane lantern.

- ☀ Focus on getting the tent up and getting lights inside it. Make sure your lights for the tent are handy. Get the little ones and the parent who is the primary caregiver inside the tent as soon as possible. Hand them your gear in the following order. Otherwise, the tent can easily get crowded with very little working space.
  - ☼ Sleeping pads
  - ☼ Sleeping bags
  - ☼ Pillows
  - ☼ Personal gear including duffle bags

Campers that arrive early get the best campsites

Bathrooms are important on campouts. So, if you do not mind being a quarter of a mile from the closest one, then go ahead and show up at 9 p.m. on a Friday night at a popular campground to get the leftover campsites. Yes, those that want the best campsites should show up early. Even if the campsite is located on private property, there are still going to be spots that are choicer than others. When you are one of the first to arrive, you get your pick of sites. While you can reserve a site ahead of time at most campgrounds, you cannot be assigned a specific site until you get there.

If you are indeed easygoing and just camping by yourself, then location might not matter that much, but if you are with your family and have little ones, proximity to the bathroom does matter. Because when those campsites are gone (occupied), they are gone for the entire weekend.

When camping with a large number families, we will often send one family up early on Friday to secure the best sites for all of us. This is especially crucial when you have multiple families and want to camp near each other. Those that arrive early get the best selection related to:

- ☀ Proximity to the bathroom
- ☀ Access to a water spigot
- ☀ Campsites with a fire ring, picnic table, lantern pole, and electricity
- ☀ Closeness to the dumpster—which is usually not the most desirable
- ☀ Access to the playground
- ☀ The best parking

Another benefit is the line at most state parks on a Friday night can get backed up. Do what it takes to leave early—take off half a day from work or leave early on Friday for weekend camping. Just do it, and you can spend more time on Friday night with your family and less time waiting in line. Also, it is sometimes almost impossible to tell if you have a bad campsite in the dark. Better to get there in the daylight and to be able to switch while other sites are still available. There have been a number of times where the park rangers assigned us a campsite, but after seeing it, we returned to the office and asked to be assigned a different one.

Last–minute errands often make your campsite setup more complicated

Panic started to set in as I headed north to Cabela's to pick up a box of Whirly Pop popcorn for the weekend's campout. It has become the tradition (one that I started) that on Friday night we would cook popcorn after we get our tent set up, and not just any popcorn but *gourmet* popcorn. But now I was starting to panic. I also needed to go to Dick's Sporting Goods to get a new instant-up-style canopy, Walmart to buy some grocery items I could not find when I did the rest of the food shopping earlier in the week, and firewood for Saturday night's campfire. Not only was I not going to be leaving by my planned 2 p.m. departure, but I was going to be hard pressed to even be on the road by 5 p.m. With Friday rush-hour traffic, we would not be at the state park until 7 p.m.— and that is if we skipped having dinner.

This very scenario has happened to me a few times, and it can easily challenge your mood. It can also cause you to make some truly regrettable decisions such as choosing not to bring something that your kids were sincerely expecting—like breakfast for Sunday morning or sand toys. Inevitably, on Saturday afternoon, one of my kids will ask, *"Where is the. . .?"* and I must answer that I ran out of time to find and pack it. While trying to be as nice as they can, their disappointment is obvious.

As I mentioned in the section on arriving at the campsite after dark earlier in this chapter, it is not that much fun to arrive after dark. Add to that spending extra time in traffic, possibly asking your family to skip dinner the night of your arrival, and leaving key equipment and supplies at home, these are all side effects of trying to run last-minute errands on the day you planned to head out.

No matter how late you have to stay up the night before, I suggest that you get all of your errands done before you go to bed. Other than topping off your gas tank and getting a bag or two of ice, do not plan on running ANY errands on your departure date.

Starting your day at sunrise has its advantages

Peaceful mornings can quickly become stressful when you decide to wake up late and have a hungry and possibly caffeine-starved crew waiting on you. While most kids and adults are probably fairly self-sufficient at home (able to pour their own juice or coffee, fix a bowl of cereal, and even cook their own eggs), they might not be able to be as independent on a campout. The juice and milk are probably buried under a number of items in the cooler (which might have a packing strap around it), there is no cupboard to casually get bowls and mugs from, no microwave, and no instant-on easy-to-use stove top. While your kids and spouse will eventually become more self-sufficient on campouts, you will need to be prepared and ready to serve them when they get up. Since the timing is critical, get up and start getting ready for them. Because they are coming and coming un-caffeinated!

My recommendation is to set your alarm (hopefully one that has a vibrate mode) and to get up before everyone else. I suggest setting out whatever you need to quietly sneak out of the tent before you go to sleep the night before. I usually set out a shirt, clean socks, and a bag with my contacts, a baseball cap, and things to wash my face with. Since it will most likely still be dark, I have my headlamp set out on top of that pile as well. When my alarm goes off, I quickly put on my shoes and get out of the tent since I genuinely need everyone else to continue sleeping while I get organized and ready for the day. Fifteen minutes later after taking care of my personal hygiene, I am ready to start working on everyone's breakfast.

The first thing I do is to get a pot of coffee brewing. The worst thing is for parents and kids that are used to coffee (and an automatic coffee maker on a timer) to have to wait for the coffee to brew. We usually use a percolator-style pot, and it does take a while to get ready—but I believe the coffee tastes better and has a fuller taste than my drip-style coffee maker at home.

The next thing I do is to get everything staged for breakfast. Orange juice and milk out on the table. Eggs cracked and ready to go on a griddle. I also set out all of the coffee related items like mugs, creamer, sugar, and spoons. And before I forget, we typically put a plastic red/white checkered tablecloth on the table with specialized clips. And because during the middle of the night, every gnat will come out and settle on the picnic table (and the plastic tablecloth), you will definitely need to get this surface cleaned off before any of your bug-phobic campers wake up.

If you choose to have bacon, this will need to be your next task. Since so many people today cook their bacon in a microwave oven, many people have forgotten that cooking bacon on a griddle is not necessarily a fast process. Therefore, you want to make sure you have planned in enough time for this and get the bacon cooked before the rest of the food. One thing that I like to do is to cut the entire 1-pound package in half and start cooking it up. Cooking bacon in smaller pieces takes less time and can make it easier to manage on the griddle. Please note that it will lose the appeal that whole-length bacon would have.

Once the coffee has been brewed and the bacon has been cooked, I can sit back and wait for my crew to wake up. When they do, I am ready to cook pancakes and eggs to order. Also, regarding timing, I cook up all of the eggs at once, and while they are eating the eggs (and the bacon), I proceed to cook the pancakes and serve them to everyone as they come off the griddle. Since pancakes have a tendency to get soggy and cold if you try to set them aside until you have enough for everyone, I prefer to serve them immediately as they come off the griddle. There are some tricks to keeping pancakes warm that I discuss in the Dutch Ovens chapter in *The Keen Camper Camping with Kids Volume 2* book.

The bottom line is that your typically angelic children and your wonderful spouse will most likely turn your peaceful morning into a stressful event if you all wake up at the same time. Everyone will be ready to eat and you still need to walk 10 minutes to the restroom to take care of any personal hygiene before you can even get started on breakfast!

As a reminder, this campout (and this breakfast) is about your family and not about you. Once again, take one for the team and get yourself up and out of bed before everyone else. It will be well worth it. Also, if you are planning on doing KP, you should get the KP line ready before they get up as well.

Dealing with a rainy forecast

Muddy and damp, and still some of the best campouts we have ever had. Sometimes camping in rainy conditions is just not avoidable. My suggestion is to almost always push forward regardless of the forecast. You might ask why. First, the forecast is not always correct and can be grossly off-target. Last year, when I headed out with a group of youth for a wilderness survival campout (which means sleeping outside in a homemade shelter without a tent), the forecast was 90 percent chance of rain all weekend, with Saturday night getting down into the mid-30s. While the mid-30s part turned out to be on the mark, it did not even begin to rain until we were all packed up and about to drive off on Sunday morning.

On another occasion, the forecast suddenly changed (for the better) during the middle of a mid-September Boy Scout campout. On Saturday morning, it started raining as predicted and did so for the next 4 hours. Even still, the group of Scouts that were with us continued to build two pioneering structures with logs and ropes. Then, just before 3 p.m. when a group of guests were scheduled to arrive to use the pioneering structures, the sky miraculously cleared and the rain stopped. The guests that made the decision to come out despite the rain had a marvelous (and dry) time. Those that chose not to come missed a wonderful experience and a fantastic dinner and campfire that followed.

There have been other campouts where one of the leaders cancelled the event halfway through the weekend due to concerns over the weather. In one case, there was actually a National Weather Service warning of legitimately dangerous weather coming. In the other case, we experienced a microburst which came in and damaged some of the group's gear and made the ground nothing but soggy. After that deluge, people were just "done." At that point, the unit leadership cancelled the campout. Well, that cheated the group of the evening campfire, Sunday church service, and wasted a lot of food that was planned for Sunday's breakfast.

What you can do is to plan every campout as though it is going to rain. Here are my recommendations:

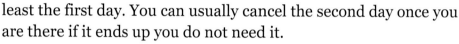

- ☀ Pack raincoats for everyone.
- ☀ Bring spare shoes for everyone.
- ☀ Bring a 10x10-foot or larger instant-up canopy.
- ☀ If camping with more than just your family, reserve the closest nearby pavilion for at least the first day. You can usually cancel the second day once you are there if it ends up you do not need it.
- ☀ Bring lots of spare clothes for the little ones.
- ☀ Pack your clothes in Ziploc-style bags so that you will always have dry clothes to change into.
- ☀ Only bring tents that you know do not leak. It is my experience that tents that have been kept in the attic during the summer months are probably the most vulnerable to leaks.

With all of this said, try your best to not stress out about the rain forecast. Be prepared and just go. Your kids and your spouse will be impressed by your carefree but yet well-prepared perspective. Some of the best campouts I have been on were ones where it was supposed to rain and didn't, rained unexpectedly and cleared up, or even ones where it rained the entire weekend.

Get to the showers before everyone else does

Time can beyond a doubt be squandered if your family chooses to take their showers at the wrong time. When it is just me and my sons, I will leave them in the tent and go take a shower late at night after they have gone to bed, first thing in the morning, or in the middle of the day. But when you are camping with your family—and especially if you are camping with little ones and your daughters—you need to get more organized.

Even the nicest state parks still have maybe one bathhouse for 30 campsites with only two to three shower stalls. Moms and daughters can easily cause a huge backup with it taking families two hours from the time they left camp to head to the shower to the time they come back. If you get in line for the showers behind a large family like mine (with several girls with long hair that needs washing), your wait could be worse.

When camping with a large group that has an evening campfire, my girls and wife take their shower supplies with them to the campfire. The second the campfire is over, they bolt to the showers. The other option is to take a shower before dinner when everyone else is busy with dinner prep. This actually works out well if you are cooking a Dutch oven meal and one person can monitor things back at the campsite while the other family members take showers. The only downside to this is that the little ones will have lots of time before bed to get filthy again and the smell of smoke from the campfire can undo a lot of the benefit of the shower.

The key thing here is to plan your shower times to be when you believe others will not be there and knowing that this will require some trade-offs. Please note that once others figure out your secret and what your family is doing, these off-peak times during the day will quickly become peak times as others start following suit.

Timing is even more important when camping with first-time campers

Timing can be really important when camping with first-time campers. While the free-spirited first-time campers might be ready to have an amazing time regardless of what comes their way, most people are fairly apprehensive and concerned about how they could possibly handle all of this camping "stuff" on their own. Even if you have a lot of individual camping experience, your family might not. Therefore, this section is very applicable to camping with them.

Since there are going to be some default challenges for any newbie, why let there be more challenges than there absolutely has to be? Mitigating for the timing-related challenges and concerns can really take the edge off the stress related to camping for the first time. Here are a few examples of things you can do as the leader of your campout.

- ☀ Camp in mild weather and eliminate concerns with freezing and overheating.
- ☀ Arrive before dark and keep the campsite setup from becoming a stressful situation.
- ☀ Arrive early and get the best campsite near whatever you prefer—the bathroom, the lake shore, or the playground.
- ☀ Get up early and start working on coffee and breakfast so that when your campers wake up, you are ready for them.
- ☀ Prepare and eat your dinner early so that it is on-time for your hungry campers and you can get KP done before it gets dark.

I think that you get the drift here. While you will not have control over everything, you do have control over quite a few things and when you choose to do those things. Help to make the experience as positive as you can. If you do a stellar job with the timing, your family will never know. You will know though by the unbelievable time they had and the fact that they want to go camping again.

There are advantages of being out of sync with everyone else

Crowds and lines—if these are things you like, then you should stop reading now. If, on the other hand, you really do not care for crowds and lines, please continue reading on. While I love people and enjoy being around others, I would rather there not be so many people at an event such that the quality is degraded. For example, do you really get any benefit from the thousands of people at an amusement park on a super busy day—other than having to wait three hours for a roller-coaster ride?

If you have the ability to camp at a non-peak or non-typical time, it can impact your campout experience in a very positive manner. Depending on how out of sync you can get from the rest of society, you might end up having an entire state park to yourself.

For example, state parks are open every day of the year but only really get used on weekends. If you can take a few days off in the middle of the week and can pull your kids out of school for a few days, you will get to enjoy a multi-hundred-acre state park in private tranquility. That is why many people love

being park hosts. Park hosts are typically retired couples who live at the state park usually rent and utility free. So why would they do this? Because the majority of the year, they get to live on a huge piece of property overlooking mountains or lakes or whatever the park might have to offer and have it all to themselves—except for the weekends from spring through fall.

If you can shift your schedule a little bit, you can do this as well. And the trade-off will be well worth it. The only real downside that I have seen is that sometimes during non-peak times you might not have access to everything—maybe the snow-cone stand will be closed, or the park office closes early, or someone is not there to rent you a canoe.

What lessons in leading your family can you take away from this aspect of camping?

"Optimal Trade-offs"

Just as in the other chapters of this book, I think there are key leadership concepts that you can (and should) take away that will help you lead your family with renewed vigor. And you will have some additional tools in your parenting/leadership toolbox. If there is a key phrase for this chapter it would be "optimal trade-offs." While these optimal trade-offs were centered solely on how to help your family have a better camping experience, I think that the concepts are easily applicable to other areas of your life. The people that I have seen who really, really have had bad camping experiences tend to have a victim mentality. They tend to see the situations that happened on the campout as only having had one outcome—which, in their case, was *not* optimal. I think many of us see this in our own families. We feel like we have very few choices and are just being carried along by the river of life. But to get past that, you have to believe that there are options beyond the ones that are being provided. Take a grocery store, for example. You go to the baking section and see two types of oils—vegetable and canola. Imagine that you have shopped at this store your whole life and that is the extent of the choices you have knowledge of. But who says those are the only choices? Those are just the only two that are being presented to you.

Let's take real-world struggles in your family. Every day you leave work headed home with the desire to work out. But like clockwork, you end up leaving late, traffic is worse than usual or expected, and when you get home, your kids need you to take them somewhere. You feel like you have no choice and you will never be able to work out. And since you used to always work out after school or after work before you had kids, you think this is your only option. What about the simple choice of working out in the morning? Yes, there is a trade-off. You will need to get up earlier, which will require you to get to bed sooner—which means there will be some things you might have to stop doing (like watching the late-night talk shows).

Take the mom who gets home from work every day and wants to feed her family delicious and healthy home-cooked meals but realizes that it is nearly impossible for them to ever be ready until almost 8 p.m. Who says she has to prepare the meals the night they will be eaten? Why can't they all be prepared at the same time on the prior weekend? Yes, you will be spending your Sunday afternoon or evening differently, but you will not have to stress out each night of the week after that. Your kids can take the meal out of the refrigerator and put it in the oven for you or you can have a slow cooker going all day. In fact, there are lots of businesses that can help you prepare these freezer meals via a Freezer Meal Workshop such as those offered by Pampered Chef consultants.

All of the areas I covered in this chapter are in response to actual stresses my family experienced early on in our camping trips. Each one initially felt like it did not have a satisfactory solution, but since we were committed to wanting to enjoy our camping experiences, we thought through the options and questioned everything. Who said you could not have your shower *before* dinner? Who said you couldn't take off work early to get your campsite set up in the daylight?

I challenge each of you to do the same with your family life. What items continue to be thorns in your family's dynamics? Make a list of them and question everything. If your car payment is causing you stress, why can't you consider selling the car, paying off the loan, and buying a lower-quality vehicle in cash? Is it really worth carrying the stress of that debt with you every day? The trade-off might be that you will be driving a "beater" instead of a luxury sedan.

Not only can you improve your family's situation, but you can also reduce the stress level in your family as well. And most importantly, your kids and spouse will see you not taking the role of victim in life's initially no-choice undesirable situations.

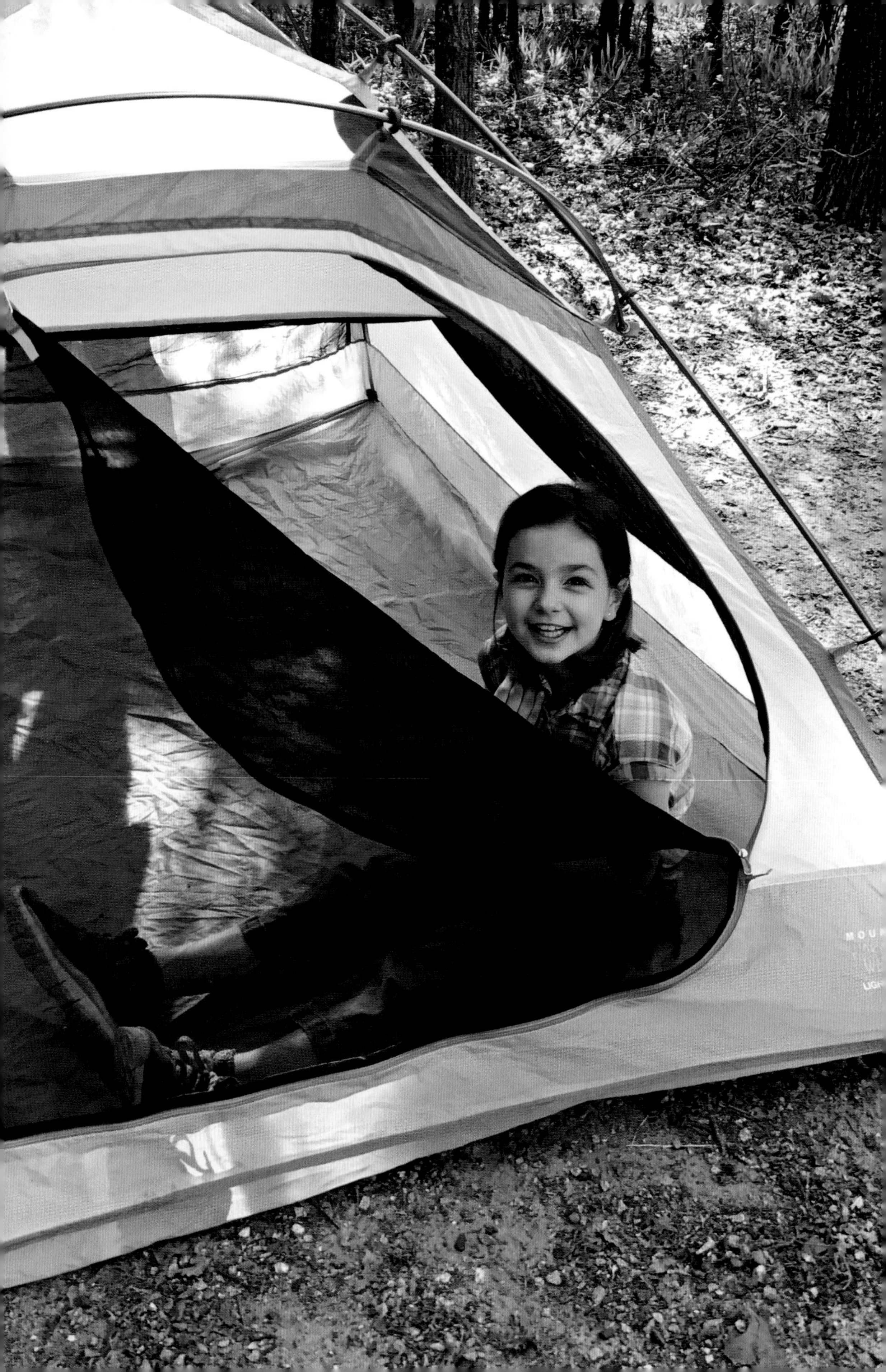

CHAPTER 4

TENTS & SHELTERS

You need to understand tent sizing before you buy a tent

Privacy and space are two things that you do not realize how important they are until you no longer have them. Therefore, it is critically important to bring the correct size tent with you on the campout. The problem is that most of us totally underestimate how much space we need. On top of that, tent manufacturers exasperate the situation with their very confusing sizing method. When you see a tent that is labeled three-person, this means it is intended for three people to sleep side-by-side with the lengths of their bodies most likely touching. With some larger-size tents that are rated for five to nine people, this can only be accomplished if some of the people are oriented perpendicular to the other sleepers. Once again, everyone's bodies will be touching, and there's not any room for individual sleeping pads—just your sleeping bags.

Why they do this, I really do not know. How is a first-time camper supposed to know that a three-person tent only sleeps two people (and barely that) and a nine-person only really sleeps six? And with these lower "actual" tent size numbers, there is still almost no room to walk between the sleeping bags or to store any personal gear.

A few years back, we were not able to show up to a Cub Scout family campout until midmorning on Saturday and ended up driving two cars since some of us were going to be spending the night and others were not. It was originally only going to be two people spending the night. Well, after I had finished packing the car, my 5-year-old daughter asked if she could spend the night too. Not wanting to get the larger seven-person tent out (and thinking about how much easier the three-person tent was going to be to put up), I said sure. We proceeded to head off with only the three-person tent. But this required that my two small children sleep on the same sleeping pad in opposite directions—one with their head near the feet of the other. After a few minutes of them pleading that they did not have enough space, they settled into the fact that Dad had not brought another tent and this was what we had. Within 15 minutes, they were both asleep

and were good-to-go. So, how could three full-size adults or teenagers fit in that three-person tent when it barely fit one adult and two children under eight years old? First, you would not have been able to use individual sleeping pads, and if you did use sleeping pads, each person would most likely have been spread across two of them. Next, you would be pressed against each other along the entire side of your body and the two people on the outsides would be touching the side of the tent as well.

Hopefully, you are getting the picture here. This is *not* how you want to camp. Having a good night's sleep and eating well are two main requirements for helping my family enjoy camping. If you mess up on this one, you have taken away 50 percent of the big knobs you can turn to help improve the camping experience.

A good rule of thumb is to reduce the manufacturer's recommendation by 33 percent. Therefore, a three-person tent would fit two people, and a nine-person tent would fit six. But even with this, you will not have much room to walk around between everyone's sleeping areas and might have to put your personal gear at the end of your sleeping pad.

Having multiple tents provides more flexibility

Once you have gone camping for the first time and actually used your tent, you will probably find out what you like and do not like about your tent. With that said, our family has multiple tents that we have purchased over several years. We have ones that range from high-dollar three-person backpacking tents to a huge (and heavy) nine-person "mansion" that is tall enough that an adult can stand completely upright in every spot in the tent (not just in the middle).

The biggest advantage of having multiple tents is the flexibility that it gives you. When it is just myself and one kid, I take the three-person backpacking tent. It takes only 5 to 10 minutes to set up, can be lifted up when you get ready to leave and shaken out, and utilizes a stuff bag for putting it away. When I bring my entire family of seven and need to have a place for each of us to sleep, room for the portable toilet, and the bunk cots, I bring the largest tent I have. Also, some of the larger tents are toilsome to set up by yourself—so if you have helpers, make sure to utilize them.

Also, since it is usually more enjoyable to camp with others, we often invite other families to camp with us. Since not everyone has a tent (or any camping gear for that matter), being able to loan someone a tent can be a real blessing. And since it is one of yours, you  will know all of the tricks and nuances of how to help them set it up.

Last, it is just really cool to have multiple tents. It really solidifies that you are a "real camper" and that you take things seriously enough that you can "shop" in your own camping equipment stash for the best tent for your specific situation.

Also, certain tents are better in certain seasons. For instance, my backpacking tent has a full coverage rainfly. Therefore, when it is on, you have very little ventilation. When it is off, you have absolutely no privacy. On the other hand, one of my large tents has a roof that is completely mesh and the rainfly does not go down very much below it. Therefore, it is very easy for rain to come in under the rainfly at the edge and get our gear wet. Still, another tent I have is a blend of both. It has a rainfly that comes down low enough to keep us dry in stormy weather but has doors and windows that have flaps that can be unzipped (leaving the mesh areas open) to provide lots of ventilation. If in the middle of the night it starts to rain or the temperature drops, all we have to do is zip that flap up versus having to go outside and try to put the rainfly on in the middle of the night.

The shape of your tent is important

As hard as it might seem, some tents will just not fit in certain campsites. When selecting a place for your tent, considerations include:

- ☀ Is it under a tree (that could have branches that could fall or scrape against the tent roof all night)?
- ☀ Are there anthills?
- ☀ Do you have enough room to extend the guy-lines for the rainfly?
- ☀ Is it in an area that will become a stream when it rains?
- ☀ Is the ground too rocky (and would puncture the bottom of your tent even with a tarp underneath it)?
- ☀ Is the ground sloped?

On a related note, at a recent summer camp we had a very large branch (probably well over 100 pounds in weight) fall from a tree during a storm one evening. It completely crushed half of a canvas-style tent. Fortunately, nobody was sleeping on that side of the tent.

With so many different potential obstacles, there is no way you will know which ones you might encounter until you reach the campsite. Therefore, having a tent with the smallest footprint is the best. A case in point—I have an interesting "first tent" (meaning, the first tent I purchased) that is L-shaped. It has always been challenging to use. First, I need two to three different-sized tarps to provide adequate coverage underneath this tent since tarps do not come in an L-shape. Just laying these out, and then adjusting and readjusting probably adds 10 minutes to our tent setup time. Then, trying to find a space that has been cleared and is ready to receive an L-shaped tent is always tough. And then to make things worse,

when I am ready to leave, trying to roll up an L-shaped tent has its own challenges. I have to remember which section of the L gets folded into the rest of the tent first, and then how to roll the entire thing up. And the rainfly for this tent is odd-shaped as well. It is not obvious how it should go on until you have almost finished putting it on (usually the wrong way).

Then, you have the huge rectangular super long tents from the retail stores—some that actually bow or lean out on the sides. Finding a big enough open spot for this style of tent can be tough too. Regarding open spots, very few places in the woods are clear enough for such large tents— especially rectangular ones. Therefore, those are best used at state parks where large tent sites have usually already been cleared and prepared for you.

Another challenging type of tent is the one with a built-in vestibule or carport. These vestibules tend to not provide a lot of real value—at least not from the living quarters aspect of the tent—but do take up a lot of extra real estate.

While many of the high-end tents can be purchased with custom-matching tarps, if the tent is asymmetrical, it can be difficult to determine how to orient the tarp—especially in the dark. A case in point is my three-person backpacking tent. The footprint is a trapezoid, and I sometimes forget whether the short or long side matches up to the entrance of the tent. If possible, make sure to get a tent whose tarp has an obvious orientation or that is symmetrical in all directions.

Tents with poles that are externally clipped on are easier to set up

In the darkness, everything tends to be more challenging and frustrating, especially when setting up a tent that you only set up a few times each year. Since I tend to do a variety of camping with different members of my family at different times, I tend to bring different tents based on the needs of the weekend. Therefore, some of my tents might only get used once a year. With that said, you quickly remember once you start "trying" to put your tent up how much you have forgotten about putting it up.

Therefore, the easier and more obvious a tent is to set up, the better. Several of the lower-end tents I have use pole sleeves. These sleeves are folded over pieces of fabric that are built into the outside top/roof of the tent or the underside of the rainfly that the shock-corded fiberglass poles go through. Sometimes (but not always), these fabric sleeves are a different color, but sometimes they are not. A few challenges—first, they tend to crisscross at a common point at the peak of the tent. This is tough because it is sometimes difficult to push them thru if there is a gap in the fabric at the meeting point. The second is that the manufacturer wants you to tie the crossing poles together at these common meeting points with a fabric cord that is attached to the tent. This can be challenging too—especially if it can only be done after the tent is up and you are not tall enough. Another challenge is that none of this is obvious in the dark or in inclement weather. And, finally, when sliding these poles through the sleeves, the meeting points of the shock-corded pole sections can catch the sleeve and when you (or your little ones) keep shoving the poles through when they get stuck (since that is our natural inclination), they catch and permanently rip the sleeves.

A much-better solution and style of tent are ones where the poles clip on the outside of the tent and are pulled up like a cantilevered trestle bridge. This design usually has the poles insert into a hole or go over a pin at the corners and crisscross loosely above the tent. At that point, a central clip is used to snap on over the common point. Then, on each side, there will be multiple clips that snap on to the poles. What is also notable about this is that newbies and kids can figure this out without any help from you. I found this out firsthand when I started to say to my 11-year-old and 9-year-old *"You need to clip. . ."* and they immediately interrupted me and said, *"Dad, we know, we know."* I guess they had been paying attention all the times we had previously put it up.

Also, a rainfly that attaches via clips that hang from its underside is the way to go as well. Many lower-priced tents only use Velcro loops on the underside of the rainfly to attach the rainfly to the tent. While nothing is wrong with having Velcro loops for extra security and stability, their use should be optional and not be "the" way to attach the rainfly.

I have seen that these clipped-on-pole style tents tend to be more expensive though. I do not know if that is because there is a patent on them or if it is simply that eight or more hard plastic clips (that are sewn to the tent) cost more than the inexpensive folded-over fabric sleeves. I suspect it is the latter, though.

The multiple benefits of tarps, footprints, and ground cloths

Timesavers are things that I am always looking for regarding my campouts. How do I organize things to be successful and more efficient? One of the items I have struggled with the most is coming home from a campout, and then needing to spend several hours cleaning and putting things away. To that end, one of the things I am often challenged by is dealing with damp tents. Even if you have a completely dry campout without any rain or visible condensation, you will still need to deal with the underside of the bottom of your tent being damp. This is primarily due to the weight in certain areas (from people sleeping and walking inside the tent) pressing down into the ground and thus, drawing the moisture

out. If the area is sandy or dirt filled, this will result in dirt/mud sticking to the underside of the bottom of your tent as well.

So imagine you have your entire campsite packed up and your tent has been taken down. All that is left is for you to fold up your tent and put it in its bag. As you start to make the first fold, you then discover the underside of the bottom of the tent is damp and has clumps of dirt stuck to it in places. You then have a couple of choices. One is to try to dry those areas as you fold up the tent. The second is just to fold it up as is. If you choose the latter, the dirt will most likely find its way back into the tent via the mesh areas. This could, in turn, lead to permanently staining the sides and roof of the tent which tend to be lighter shade colors and not as heavy duty as the tent floor.

The best solution for this is to always put an inexpensive tarp underneath your tent. Yes, you will still have the same issue, but the dirt and moisture will be on the bottom of a tarp that can be dealt with later or hung out to dry while you complete the rest of your packing—instead of being on the bottom of a high-dollar tent.

Another side benefit is that the tarp will take the brunt of the wear and tear and not the bottom of your tent. It is much more practical to replace a tarp

or to repair it with duct tape than to have to replace or repair an entire tent due to holes in the floor. This is especially important since it is very difficult at times to find a location for your tent that does not have rocks or tree roots. These obstacles can easily punch a hole in your tent (if you are not using a tarp) when a person stands on them.

Another benefit is preventing any seepage of water from the rain coming through the bottom of the tent. This is not true for most large tents that have heavy-duty tarp-like floors but is an issue for lighter-weight backpacking-style tents with floors that are made out of the same material as the sides and roof. Water can seep through if there is enough water between the tent bottom and the ground. While some rain runoff will get between the tent and the tarp, most of it will run off between the ground and the tarp.

Lately, many tent manufacturers are offering "footprints" that are the exact size and shape of the tent they are made for. This greatly improves the ease of putting down a tarp. The only real downside is the cost. In some cases, these footprints can cost as much as 15 percent of the cost of the tent. Please note that you will occasionally see the term "ground cloth" used interchangeably with the terms tarp and footprint.

Finally, if you do use a traditional-style tarp, make sure to come back and fold in the edges of the tarp. You want all of the tarp tucked under the tent. If not, then any rain that lands on this extra area of the tarp (that is hanging out from underneath the tent) will run directly under the tent. Due to the potential amount of water that could be drawn under your tent, this might lead to seepage issues. Even if you do not have seepage issues, you will definitely have a wet tent bottom to deal with when you get ready to fold-up the tent at the end of the campout.

Window and rainfly designs impact ventilation and rain protection

Miserable is not a word you want associated with the time you spend in your tent—especially at night. Most of us end up buying generic all-season tents because we do not know there are any other options. While these all-season tents will *work* in all-weather situations, they do not thrive at the ends of the spectrum. And these shortcomings can result in us being less-than-happy campers. While you want to have protection from the elements, you also do not want to be so bundled-up and snuggled-down to the point that your tent is more like a Native American teepee sweat lodge.

You definitely want a tent that has a vented roof with a sufficient space between it and the rainfly. As hot air rises, this gap will provide a path for the hot air to escape. By the same token, if you have a vented ceiling but do not have a rainfly, all of the warmth (that you need on colder nights) will quickly escape out of the tent. This design also allows sinking cold air to pour in through the vented ceiling and to settle inside your tent at the ground level where you are sleeping. Therefore, you really do not want your roof to be the only ventilation that you have. My preference is to have dual-layer doors. A dual-layer door has mesh on the outside and standard tent material on the inside. The mesh part is a permanent part of the tent, while the inside layer can be zipped up or down as needed. If it is a hot evening, you can partially unzip the flap, leaving the mesh panel exposed. If in the middle of the night, you wake up cold, all you need to do is to zip the flap/door all the way up. My preference would also be to have two mesh openings at opposite sides of the tent to allow for cross ventilation. This could be two doors, a door and a window, or two windows.

While I often see people not put up their rainflys, I tend to think this is not the best choice. It could rain out of nowhere and those individuals will end up with all of their gear getting soaked. Therefore, when you are selecting your tent, ask yourself what openings are available to manage the ventilation and cross flow of air in your tent.

Tent ceiling canopies and hooks/rings provide extra benefits

Losing an item in your tent like your car keys or stepping on your only pair of sunglasses can quickly steal your campout joy. No matter how organized you try to be, there are still going to be times when you decide to unzip your tent and to throw your car keys or sunglasses on your sleeping bag. Because of how tight the sleeping arrangements are in tents, there is a reasonable chance your tentmates (and especially your kids) will step on your sleeping bag. I have seen this result in broken glasses or even more troublesome—lost car keys (that were accidentally kicked  off your sleeping bag) that are now under the mess of gear in your tent. This problem can easily be solved by getting a tent with a hanging mesh canopy that can be hung from the ceiling. My favorite style is the one with the pocketed flaps that hang down. If you are having trouble imagining this canopy, think of it as a mini mesh hammock for your small pocket-sized gear that hangs from the ceiling of the tent. These provide a way to keep your must-have small items off the ground. And as a reminder, since your sleeping bag is on the ground, any gear you set on it is essentially on the ground as well.

Please note that in some higher-end tents, these canopies can cost as much as 25 percent of the cost of the tent—seriously! If provided, mesh side pockets on each side wall are a reasonable alternative as well for your small items.

Also, while in your tent at night, you really do need a sufficient amount of light that is preferably installed at the highest point in your tent. If not installed high enough, you can have all sorts of shadow-related lighting issues. From these same loops that we just discussed for hanging mesh canopies from, you can also clip on a carabiner that you can subsequently hang lights from. While I have several higher-dollar camping and tent lights, my favorite is an inexpensive LED light that is pictured on page 179. These are super bright (until the batteries run down), lightweight, and are readily available.

A tent doormat is a necessity

While I have had a few people laugh at me for bringing a doormat for my small backpacking tent, I still swear by it. For my small tent, there is a small vestibule area right outside the tent. Since the tent is so small, the easiest way to get things in and out of it is to kneel down and reach back into the tent across

my sleeping bag while lying on my stomach. I do not like to be bothered having to remove my shoes, and I do not want to have to kneel down in the dirt right in front of the tent door. This is where my doormat comes in handy. I just kneel down on it.

For my larger tent, we typically use it to put shoes and flip-flops on—yes, my kids sometimes bring flip-flops on campouts. This area serves two main purposes. First, it helps us keep everything more orderly and organized. Second, it provides a place for us (and especially my kids) to sit down to put their shoes back on after leaving the tent.

The key is to purchase a doormat that is super thin so that it can be rolled up for easy transportation to the campsite. It should be solid and without holes since it will be placed directly on the dirt. Also, make sure to pack an extra black garbage bag that you can put this rolled up doormat in when you head home since it will undoubtedly be dirty.

Here is an interesting side story about the first two camping doormats I purchased. Originally, I went to a home improvement store and was able to purchase a huge 4x3-foot size doormat. When I got ready to buy the smaller (half size) version at the same store the next day, it was twice the price. I guess that nobody was buying the large ones and that is why they were put on sale. Since I already had in my mind what the small mat should have cost, it was very hard for me to now "overpay" for it—especially since I had already paid less for the same style larger version.

While I have seen others bring rolled up carpet instead of a doormat, these tend to get very dirty and are hard to keep clean. Therefore, go with a doormat that can be easily hosed off at home in between your camping trips instead.

Make sure to pack a mallet and tent stake puller

There have been several times that I have been tempted when space was tight in either my car or my personal gear bag (when traveling with others) to not bring my rubber mallet. Thank goodness I have never knowingly given in to that temptation.

Because each time we camp, we tend to do so at places we have never camped before, we never know the condition of the ground and whether it will be soft enough to push tent stakes in by hand. You might say, *"Well, I can just stomp them in."* While I do not know the ins and outs of why it works this way, when you try to put a tent stake into the hard ground with your foot, it will tend to bend—especially if it is shaped like a candy cane. When using a rubber mallet,

I do not recollect this ever happening. And absolutely, do not give in to the temptation to not stake your tent to the ground. If a strong wind starts to blow, your tent (even with your gear in it) can, and will, fly away. It is possible, though, to not tie down every rainfly cord if the fly has another mechanism to keep it taut based on how it is attached to the tent's poles.

The next issue is when you get ready to leave. Those tent stakes that you worked so hard to get into the ground often do not want to come back up. Some of them will seize up as though they were screwed into a wooden tree root. While

I have used dedicated tent peg pullers, they tend to bend when the going gets tough and end up being useless. My preference is to install a very heavy-duty J-hook at the end of the handle of my mallet. This provides one tool to do both jobs. Occasionally, the mallets found in the camping section of retail stores will have this J-hook already installed.

The only real downside to bringing a mallet is where to pack it in your gear. Especially if you are trying to put it in a backpack and do not want the J-hook to catch on things such as clothes. Additionally, make sure to put your name on the mallet handle with a permanent marker. It seems that most campers do not bring mallets (or small brooms and dustpans either). After you loan it out, it will most likely get passed between all of those who did not bring a mallet either. After the last person uses it, they will not know who it belongs to and will just set it down somewhere. At least by labeling it, there is a chance you might see it again. As a side note, the top three items I am continually asked to loan out on campouts are (1) a can opener, (2) a broom & dustpan, and (3) my rubber mallet.

The best place to set up your tent

Most people do not think about campouts as being fatal, but there is a slight risk of death if you do not set up your tent in the most optimal place. Recently, I heard in the news about some hikers that set up their campsite at the very bottom of a valley. Later that night, there was a flash flood (due

to a large amount of rain) that swept them and their tents away. I believe that none of them survived. Several years before, at a National Boy Scout Jamboree, a boy died while helping to set up a dining fly when one of the taller metal poles touched an overhead power line. There are also many stories of branches falling on tents and subsequently crushing those sleeping inside the tent. Since trees in the woods are typically not monitored, pruned, or trimmed, there is just no telling which trees are on their last leg and which ones are healthy and will be rock solid for many years to come.

So, the first concern is from things overhead—power lines, tree branches, and falling rocks. The second concern is things on the ground such as anthills, rotting trees, rocky ground, root-infested areas, low elevation, and sloping ground. The anthills and rotting trees (with their associated insects) are pretty important to consider while the low elevation ground could potentially be deadly if water comes your way. Rocky, root-infested, and sloping ground are more comfort-level concerns than safety ones.

Regarding the sloping ground, I almost always take a minute to lay down on the tarp before proceeding any further. I want to make sure that where I am planning to place my head in the tent is elevated relative to the rest of my body. It is no fun to realize when you lay down to sleep for the night that all of your blood is rushing toward your head because it is lower than your feet. Not thinking about this ahead of time and accidentally setting things up so that your head is on a downward incline can impact your night's sleep. While using a pillow can help mitigate against this, the best option is to keep your body on a slope with your feet being lower than your head. If you are in a tent by yourself, this is easy to fix—just flip yourself around. If you are in a tent with others, this might not be so easy. First, you might need to rotate 90 degrees, which might not be possible based on how your tenting partner have their spaces laid out. Second, while you can almost always rotate 180 degrees, your roommate might not appreciate (especially if you start off lying on top of your sleeping bag) having your feet near his or her face.

When selecting a place to put your tent, here are some points to consider:

- ☀ In an open spot.
- ☀ Not near a field or clearing (due to the wind).
- ☀ Not near a body of water with no trees in between (due to the wind).
- ☀ Nothing above you that could fall and harm you.
- ☀ Not at the bottom of a culvert.
- ☀ In a place where the most number of people in the tent can have their heads elevated.

How you store your tent will impact its lifespan

On the campout in the middle of the night during a thunderstorm is *not* when you want to realize that your tent is no longer water repellent. I have seen this happen too many times. Once to me when a tent I had been given started leaking. On a separate occasion, I saw a family pack up and leave after one night (much to their kid's dismay) after their first campout in years was "ruined" in their minds when their tent (which had always been stored in their attic in the heat of Texas) started leaking. While climates are very different in various parts of the country, it is probably safe to say that putting camping gear in your home's attic is like leaving it out in the elements (related to heat and cold). Fortunately, a substantial number of people in the north have basements which provide a sizeable place to store camping gear.

While some newer style high-tech tents utilize fabric that has been engineered to be water repellent, most of the older and more inexpensive ones use a sprayed-on water repellent coating. While this coating will hold up for some years, it will eventually lose its effectiveness. If your tent is exposed to extreme heat (such as that in your attic), the rate of its deterioration will be much faster.

Thus far, I have not found a way to test whether a tent is really water repellent short of setting it up, and then spraying it down with water. Therefore, if your tent ends up leaking on a campout, your best option is to discard it either at the campsite or immediately after you get home. While I have seen some people respray their tents (and especially the rainfly) with a water-repellent coating, I just do not think it is worth the risk. Do not fool yourself into believing that your tent might not leak the next time it rains on a campout.

Do not bring damaged or leaking tents on campouts

Shortsighted is the best way to describe someone who would knowingly bring a damaged or leaking tent on a campout. While I love people and try to do my best to never criticize or put others down, I need to apologize ahead of time for the following rant. Knowingly (and that is the *key* word) bringing a damaged tent or one that is known to not hold back water is just foolish. I once heard the definition of a fool as being someone who does not do anything different but somehow expects different results. Regarding this rant, I am calling out the person that already knows that the tent will leak if it rains but just hopes it will not. I am also calling out the person that knows that the broken fiberglass tent pole has been duct-taped together but would like to believe it will hold-up a little longer. We need to live in the world of what-is (where you admit you really need a new tent) and not the world of what-if (hoping that everything will hold-up just a little bit longer). That's the end of my rant. I 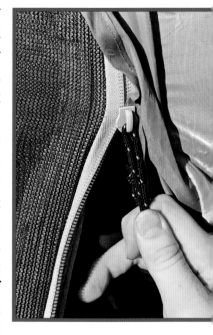 have seen too many kids and adults negatively impacted by the primary "camping" parent bringing a tent that was not up-to-par on the campout. It is really hard seeing kids having to go home early because of their parents' poor judgment.

Do not get me wrong—I am very sensitive and concerned about the camping experience being affordable, but let's put this in perspective. Consider a brand-new eight to nine-person Ozark Trail tent from Walmart for $90, gas to and from the campout is probably going to run you $20, the campsite fee is probably $20/day, and the food you brought for a family of four or five is $100. So, let's say your budget for the weekend is $160, and you end up having a terrible time after your tent collapses or leaks (and everything gets soaked). If you bought a new tent, the cost would go up to $250. So, do you want to spend $250 and greatly reduce your risk from this situation or stay at $160 and have the possibility you will need to leave the campout early and that a significant amount of that $160 might be wasted?

A few years back, we were camping with a group of Cub Scout families and had to be emergency evacuated to a storm shelter. We had all gone to our tents for the evening when the assistant park ranger frantically drove up to our site and found my tent and said *"I need you to get everyone out of their tents and immediately go to the old dining hall."* We quickly woke everyone up and all headed across a large open field in the dark toward our destination—some of us carrying our little ones in the rain. Shortly after that, it hit. The wind gusts were close to 60 mph, and the rain was coming in sideways. Since it was dark, we just assumed that our campsite was going to be a total loss and that our tents and personal gear would be strewn everywhere. After a few hours, we were given the all-clear to return to what was left of our campsite. Much to our surprise, all but two of the 24 tents were still standing. We found out that one of those two actually belonged to one of our den leaders. It turned out he had set up his tent using broken tent poles that were duct-taped together. Subsequently, he and his son ended up spending the rest of the night sleeping in their car. The next morning, the rest of us were able to peacefully enjoy our Sunday breakfast and worship service, and then casually pack up. The den leader and his son, on the other hand, had not slept well, were still in wet clothes, had no dry clothes, and still had an hour-plus drive home.

Several years ago, I thought I was being blessed when a friend offered to give me a free tent that was "just" missing a single pole. I ended up spending a lot of effort getting this five-person tent operational again. After much research and failed attempts to buy a replacement pole (since, according to Coleman, this tent did not exist), I was able to get it functional again. The tent worked flawlessly for the next several campouts until the first time it rained (and it leaked). The first time it rained, I thought it was because it had rained all weekend and at times at a torrential pace. And even though it leaked a second time, I still had my son and his friend use it one more time. And guess what? It leaked a third time! I eventually threw the entire tent away. It was tough to do due to the emotional and time investment I had made in repairing it. But the point of a campout is not to take pride in the accomplishment of getting a tent operational again but instead, to help others have the best experience possible. If you have a broken or leaking tent, just get rid of it and start fresh. You will be glad that you did.

Prepare for the (un)expected – What should be in your repair kit?

With kids on a campout, you need to be prepared for anything and the possibility that your tent will get damaged. While most campout issues can be worked around pretty easily or via a quick trip into town and possibly even to Walmart, when you have tent issues, it can be a big deal. Especially if your tent is already up and fully loaded. Yes, you could buy another tent but transferring everything from one tent to another and having to spend your hard-earned money on a spontaneous tent purchase is probably something you would like to avoid.

The tent issues that I have seen the most tend to be zipper related. Another is pole related, and the third is hole/tear related. Having the right supplies with you can change these from trip-ending events to minor bumps in the road. Kids love to go in and out of your tent all day long. They cannot help it—they are kids, and that is how they are wired. Once you get them to finally start zipping it up each time, you are then faced with the issue of the zipper eventually getting jammed or coming off the track. There are three things that will help when this happens: (1) a seam ripper, (2) a small pair of scissors, and (3) a pack of snap-on zipper pulls. If a zipper comes off the track, the easiest thing to do is to rip out the sewn-in stop and try to rethread the zipper pull. At the location you cut, you can usually put the zipper pull back on. You can just be careful to not unzip it past that point, or you can take a threaded needle and loop it around the end of the zipper several times to create a stop.

If the zipper is completely jammed, you can try folding the piece of material that is jammed to the side and try to move the zipper up and down until the material is freed up. If that will not work, you have the option of using a snap-on zipper pull.

A few years ago, I found these near the checkout lane of a craft store. The pack was very affordable and came with an assortment of styles and sizes. Since they come in two pieces (front and back) that snap together, these are not heavy-duty. But they can be snapped in place just past the point where the original zipper pull is jammed. This will give you the ability to zip up your tent and to make it through the campout. Cutting the material stuck in the zipper pull with your scissors can also be done, but the damage you do to the tent at that location will be more difficult, or impossible, to fix later.

The next issue is poles. Two main issues I have seen are broken or stretched shock cord or a broken fiberglass pole. I have fiberglass repair tape that I bring that is intended to repair broken shovel handles. This will at least get you through the rest of the campout. Regarding the shock cord, you can stretch out a piece and insert an overhand knot into it to make things tighter again. While you can bring extra shock cord, just be warned that feeding it through the very tiny hole in the tent pole (unless you have a very specialized rod with a barb on the end of it) is almost impossible. While one of these "feeder" rods would be something good to have on a Boy Scout trailer, it is not practical to bring on a family campout due to its length and the sharp barb on the end.

The last issue is holes in the tent. It is pretty easy to fix a small hole with Tenacious-brand tape. I usually carry the tape in the colors of my tents. Make sure to cut two exact size pieces—one for the inside and one for outside of the tent—with both having rounded edges.

One time, we got ready to set up our tent and realized that we had a hole the size of a penny in the side of the tent. We determined that the last time we had taken down the tent, a rock had been left inside. That rock, which had sharp edges and was no more than the size of a small coin, had punctured a hole in the tent when the tent had been rolled up tight enough to fit in the tent bag. We then remembered that we were in a hurry the last time we used this tent due to a forced weather-related evacuation and made the mistake of pulling up the tent stakes before we had swept it out. When a strong wind came by, the tent started to fly away. We quickly (with the help of others) subdued it and removed the poles and proceeded to roll-up the tent up. We intended to unroll it at home and repack it. While that obviously did not happen, I now have more experience with repairing holes in tents.

Practice setting up the tent at home

Tents should look sturdy when put up and worthy of keeping you and your family safe from the elements on your camping trip. Getting a tent to look this way does not happen by accident. A few years ago, I saw a television show about a family that would take their children on practice runs to the grocery store. These were runs where they were not under a deadline to get done by a certain time or to get a certain amount of groceries. The sole intention was to walk through the store, aisle by aisle, talking to the kids about how to behave in the store, how to interact with others, and how to handle the items they were planning to buy. And, yes, they did buy a few items (primarily  snacks to reward the kids) when they were done. The point was that they did not wait until a real grocery store trip to teach their kids how to behave in the store. Instead, they chose to practice.

I would suggest that you do the same with your tent. On a reasonable weather day before your camping trip, go ahead and set up your tent in your backyard. If your garage is large enough, you can even do it in the comfort of your garage. You should feel completely comfortable before you leave for the campout on how to identify what poles go where, how the rainfly goes on, and any other nuances of your tent. If this is the first time you have set up this tent, you should verify it is complete and in working order with no tears or jammed zippers. This will also provide you the opportunity to understand what types of hooks or rings are attached to the ceiling that could be used to hang lights from. The big item that is next (which is usually not considered fun) is learning how to properly take your tent down and getting the tent, poles, stakes, and rainfly, back in the original bag. And you need to do this without ripping the tent bag or messing up the bag's zipper (due to the tent not being folded up small enough).

Also, if you are used to setting up your tent with the help of others, try putting it up by yourself if you will not have any assistance at an upcoming campout. If you are going to be setting up the tent in the dark, it might be helpful to set it up only using headlamps (or whatever your family typically uses for lighting sources on a campout) in your garage with the lights out. Make sure not to use a propane lantern if you are going to have the garage door shut though!

While I had always camped with my children on Cub Scout campouts, when my son started camping with the Boy Scouts and tenting with other boys, I was faced with the challenge of setting up my tent by myself. And the first time I attempted to do this was in the dark wearing a headlamp. I quickly realized that this was going to be challenging due to the height of the tent and the coordination required to put multiple tent poles in multiple pins/rings—at the same time. I did end up getting help, and it all worked out. But before the next campout, I purchased myself a small, easy-to-set-up backpacking tent.

The bottom line is to make sure you feel comfortable putting up your tent with the helpers you will have on the campout. Gain confidence by practicing at home. If your kids are like mine, they will eagerly volunteer to set up the tent at home so that they can hopefully play in it afterward. In fact, you will probably have some difficulties getting them to vacate it so that you can take it down later.

Instant-up canopies provide protection from the elements

While the bulk of this chapter focused on tents, I want to mention about instant-up-style canopy shelters. If you have sufficient space and money, I recommended purchasing a canopy. While 10x10-foot models abound everywhere and are usually an affordable price, please consider getting a 12x12-foot one if you can. The magic is in the math. A 10x10-foot is 100 square feet while a 12x12-foot is 144 square feet. So, for the 2 feet more in each direction, you get almost 50 percent more space. Within a 12x12-foot space, you can easily sit ten people in camp chairs underneath it or have all of your cooking equipment covered, or possibly even a picnic table.

When buying a canopy, purchase a name-brand one that has accessories. A key accessory is the removable solid (non-mesh) sides that stop the wind and keeps the early-morning or evening sun (that comes in from the horizon) from baking you from a side opening. Also, purchase horseshoe/disc-style weights in case you are not able to stake the canopy down. These are extremely helpful when trying to put the canopy over a picnic table on an underlying cement platform or on a paved driveway where an RV would normally go. These weights are also vital when the ground is too rocky or hard to accommodate tent stakes.

Another feature is to get one with a vented top to allow hot air to escape but prevents rain from coming in. If you can find and afford it, you should also consider purchasing mesh screen sides. For the screen sides, purchase ones for all four sides; otherwise, what is the point? For the solid sides, you usually only need one or two. If you have more than that, you have essentially created a hot sauna, which I am sure, is not your goal. For the mesh sides, you are trying to enclose the entire structure (from bugs).

If space is not an issue, you can also buy very affordable portable carports. These use solid steel poles and can provide a tremendous amount of coverage, sometimes up to 12x20-foot. The downsides are the size, weight, storage, transportation, and the extra time and care it takes to set it up.

The reason for these canopies is two-fold. Protection from the rain and protection from the sun. If you place your canopy on a hard surface (that will not get muddy), you can camp all weekend in the rain and still have an enjoyable time—but having that dry base is critical. Also, trying to prepare or eat lunch in the direct sunlight is a real beating. Therefore, a canopy can make a huge difference by providing you shelter from the sun.

Lastly, consider finding a string of LED lights to go underneath your canopy.

A set that can work off either AC electricity or via battery would be the preferred option and would give you the most flexibility.

What lessons in leading your family can you take away from this aspect of camping?

"Expect the Expected"

The main theme of this chapter is really what I would characterize as "Expect the Expected." Even if you are a free-spirited person, you have to admit that sometimes unexpected and even bad things happen. Do we need to go around being afraid of these things, or even worse, avoid trying new things that could have undesirable, negative consequences? The answer is "no." But you do need to "expect the expected." You are probably thinking, *"doesn't he have that phrase wrong? Isn't it expect the unexpected?"* Several years ago, I wondered why, when my kids were sick, our pediatrician could always see them the same day—100 percent of the time. But when my wife or I called our ENT (Ear, Nose, Throat) doctor, the earliest he could see us was weeks out. After talking to the pediatrician's receptionist, I finally understood. The doctor knew (like it or not) that kids were going to get sick, and that sick kids needed to see the doctor fairly urgently. He also knew that kids need to see him for regular checkups—but that those appointments were not urgent. So, he purposely reserved 75 percent of his day for sick kids. Because of this, when you called him to schedule a checkup appointment, you'd have to wait over a month. He expected the expected. He knew that kids would get sick and that these requested appointments would happen at the last minute without warning.

Let's take one of the examples I mentioned earlier about the campers who drowned in a flash flood. It is going to rain, and there will be flash floods. Floods that come suddenly and unexpectedly without warning. So without being pessimistic, ask yourself, *"Where would I want my tent if the worst were to happen? Is there a location that is safer than others?"* Expect the expected.

In your own family, how much leadership do you show with expecting the expected? Do you hope that your car will not eventually need its brakes replaced, or do you plan and budget for that cost now? Do you honestly believe the dishwasher is going to last forever? If not, what is your plan for when a new one is needed? I know that most people are going to say, *"Well, money is tight, and we do not have the funds to save for it."* How hard would it be to take the cost of your dishwasher, divide it by how many months you need it to last, and then set that money aside each month? Yes, it might mean you need to go to four fewer movies with your family (of four) each year—but wouldn't it be worth it in the long run?

Let's take a nonfinancial example. You know that kids are curious and will eventually come across information on the Internet that might not be appropriate for them. Do you just tell yourself that this will not happen, or that they will use sound judgment? What about expecting the expected? That, eventually they will (either on purpose or accidentally) come across content that is not the best for them. If you really expect this to happen, have you taken steps to prevent or lessen the impact when it does? I have a friend that only lets his family use electronic devices downstairs in the main living area so that everyone can see what everyone else is looking at. I have another friend that disables his Wi-Fi access from 11 p.m. to 6 a.m. each day. They are expecting the expected.

One final example. Every day kids and pets go missing. Like it or not, it just happens. One of the local pet shops in our area has recommended that all of its customers create a "Lost Pet" flyer with all of the details about their pet. They recommend doing it now and not after your pet has gone missing. Then, if your pet does go missing, this PDF file can be posted on Facebook and other social media outlets immediately.

So, as you reflect back on this chapter and my recommendations for how to keep your family safe at night and how to help them experience a great night's sleep, what areas in your family's home life can you do the same? Where are you unrealistic because it does not seem fun to think through possible bad situations? The time to start "expecting the expected" is now.

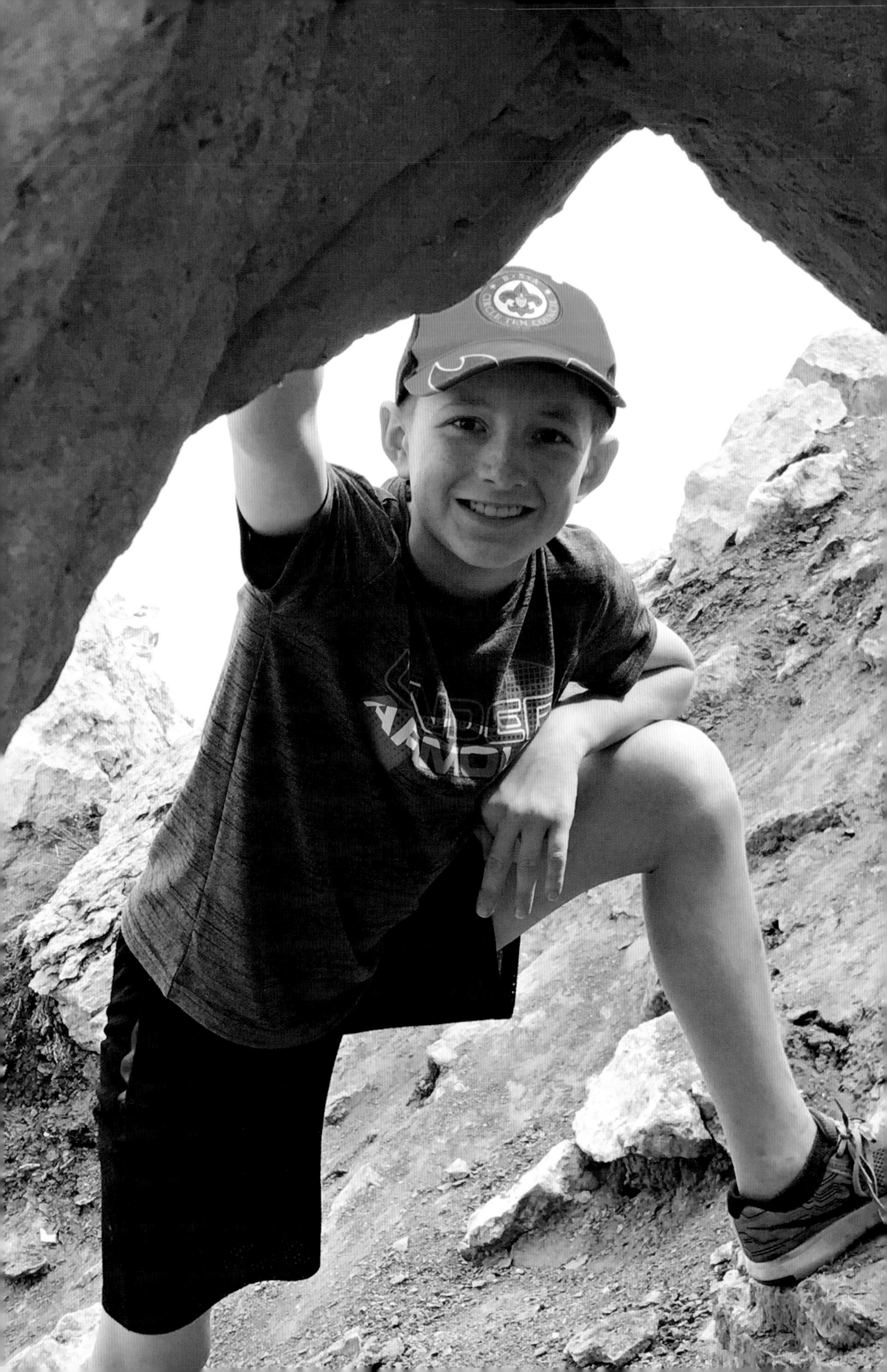

CHAPTER 5

CHECKLISTS, PACKING & GETTING THERE

Starting a staging pile days ahead makes packing easier

The choice is yours. You can either put in the effort up front, or you can scramble on the day of the campout. When we do weekend camping, I usually start to pull gear together on the Tuesday evening before a weekend campout, and then get everything finished up on Thursday evening.

Like many people, I tend to be either an optimist (and believe the packing will not take that long), or I am just a blatant denier and do not want to admit it. With that said, I suggest that you go to bed the night before your campout with everything except for your ice chest ready to be loaded up in the car. Then, on Friday afternoon, all that you must do is to load up your ice chest with your food and ice (that hopefully, you bought the day before) and load up the car. This way, you can peacefully pull out of your driveway at the time you had planned to head out for the weekend.

Since you will be camping for a relatively short amount of time versus the amount of effort you put into the overall experience (which includes getting ready and putting everything away), you really want it to count. You also want to be as relaxed as you can when you get there—having arrived when you planned to, having not forgotten anything, and having planned for any meals you might need for the day you arrive.

So, go ahead and stage an area in your garage to start putting your weekend camping gear as you gather it. Put your checklist near that staging area as well as a pad of paper and a pen (to use to capture items not on your checklist). As you pack items, scratch them off your list. As you realize you need things that are not on your list, just write them on the pad of paper. If you need to buy things, add those to that impromptu list as well. If you start this process on the Tuesday evening before your campout, it will really help to distribute the work across multiple days. Otherwise, on Thursday night you might need to run errands to multiple places. And, if these places happen to already be closed for the evening, this will force you to run these errands the day you leave—which is not the best idea.

Have your camping gear organized and stored together at home to make packing simpler

I hate to admit it, but for a few years, my camping gear was stacked in a pile in the corner of a room in my house. Unlike when you make a deliberate decision to buy something like a couch or pool table, I never said to myself, *"Let's start buying and collecting camping gear."* It just happened. I am glad that it did just happen because if I had asked myself whether I had space, I probably would have answered "no". That might have ended our hobby of family camping right then and there. Instead, I took the approach of buying what we needed. After a few years, I realized that while we very much liked family camping that something had to change. The first step was to get rid of camping gear that we were not using or only used infrequently.

After reflecting on how I could best store all of our camping gear, I realized that I could repurpose a large walk-in storage room that was currently full of other items. While the items presently in this room were still special to me, I decided that they were not as important as my camping gear. Admitting to myself that I could not keep everything was tough, but in the long run, it has been well worth it.

In this repurposed room, we installed floor-to-ceiling, wall-to-wall adjustable shelving. This allowed me to store similar items together. I had shelves for sleeping bags, shelves for sleeping pads, a shelf for mess kits, an area for rain gear, a box with flashlights & headlamps, and even a box for hygiene-related items. Now, when we go camping, my kids take an empty box or plastic crate and go "shopping" in this room. If we have three people going, we pull three sleeping bags. If we have two people going, we pull two mess kits and two Eagle brand mugs. I think you get the idea. A real side benefit of this is that my kids love this shopping aspect. When my little one was just four, she was even able to help "shop" for camping gear herself. Another side benefit is that my kids and wife have now developed a better sense of how to get ready for a campout. By helping with the packing aspect, they now know what to bring.

Another idea that I have seen is always to have a duffle bag or backpack that is always already packed. If someone says, *"Let's go camping,"* all that you need to do is to grab it and go. If you choose this method, you will need to switch out your clothes seasonally and watch the expiration dates of your hygiene items. A challenge with this concept is that if you do not get and pack a bag for every family member, you could find yourself constantly borrowing items from one bag and moving it to another, depending on who specifically is going on a specific camping trip.

The bottom line is that if you can get organized via one of these two methods, it will make your camping packing experience much easier. Also, I recently heard about families with RVs always keeping their gear in the RV. They even keep "camping clothes" stored in their RV, which are brought out when they are being worn or cleaned. This approach obviously works better for adults who are typically the same size year after year.

Using colored ribbons to identify your gear

This next idea came from my father. While not initially intended for camping, it has helped me to keep track of my gear when camping with others. After 22 years as a pilot in the United States Air Force, my father flew commercially for over a decade taking passengers all around the world. As a pilot, he would take a roll-aboard style suitcase and a flight bag on every flight. But since the pilots at his airline purchased their items at the same company store, everyone's roll-aboard and flight bag looked the same. As you can imagine, what a mess it would be if a pilot accidentally de-boarded the plane with another pilot's gear. The way that he and other pilots solved this was to tie an approximately 18-inch long bright colored ribbon to the handle of all of

their travel items. My father's color was bright orange. His ribbon came from a roll of bright orange one-inch wide heavy-duty fabric ribbon he purchased at a fabric store. I followed suit, and whenever I am waiting at the luggage carousel after a flight, it is very easy to spot my black suitcases because they all have an attached bright orange ribbon. When I started traveling for work, I continued this approach but also extended it to my laptop bag and backpack because there were too many times that my travel mates had the same ones.

Now let's move on to how this relates to camping. When my oldest son went on his first Boy Scout campout, it was a different experience for us than in Cub Scouts, where we had brought our car filled with our gear. There was no confusion about which gear was ours since it was always in our possession. For this campout, we were dropped off by my wife in the parking lot of a sporting goods store. Since the person we were riding with already had his car filled with his gear, our gear was loaded on the troop's enclosed trailer. Now, fast-forward to 3 hours later when we arrived at the campground. It was pitch black, the air already dipping down into the upper 40s, and Scouts have unloaded all of the personal gear (for 50+ people) into one massive pile so that they could get to the troop's camping gear. From there, you would find your stuff bit by bit and eventually realize that your sleeping pad is not there. The one that you bring each time and have worked hard to keep in good condition is now gone. Someone else had taken it. It was probably already in their tent where they were using it to get a good night's sleep. The problem with this entire approach was that these Scouts shopped at the same stores and had the same identical gear. And with most people not being very detail oriented, your property was gone for the duration of the campout.

That was the last time that my gear was not marked with a ribbon. Now, every single piece of large camping gear is marked with a ribbon, and my family's color is orange—just like our travel luggage. I have the following marked:

- ☀ Sleeping bags (connected to the drawstring on the stuff bag)
- ☀ Sleeping pad (connected to the storage bag itself)
- ☀ Camping chairs
- ☀ Backpacks
- ☀ Day packs

While probably not required, I do double knot the ribbon in the middle to reduce the chance of it coming off. Not only does this help me find my items, but it will also usually keep someone else from walking away with mine once they see the colored ribbon. Whenever I tell people about this marking strategy, I let them know in a somewhat joking manner that I have staked a claim to orange for my family. If they like this idea, they are welcome to use it but should choose a different color (or two colors) for their family. Thus far, none of our camping friends have been bold enough to use orange.

Now, here is where life gets just a bit more complicated. My oldest son and I have the same gear (sleeping pads, sleeping bags, tents, and gear bags), and on campouts, I prefer to put up the tent that has primarily been used by me since I know what condition it was in when we last camped. But both of these tents have the same orange ribbon on them and are not easily distinguishable. Therefore, I have marked my gear with a separate purple ribbon in addition to the orange one. Presently, I only have this on my tent since I do not care as much about which sleeping bag I get.

Use a trailer hitch basket to provide more packing capacity

Obviously, everyone's vehicles have a fixed amount of capacity, and quite often, that capacity is not enough to transport all of the gear we want to bring on a campout. One of the easiest and most cost-effective options to get a little more space is to utilize a trailer hitch basket. A trailer hitch basket is a tray that is usually 18 inches deep, 40-60 inches wide, and 6-8 inches tall that has a square rod mounted at the bottom that can be slid into your vehicle's trailer hitch female receptacle. Based on my experience, female trailer hitch receptacles come standard on most trucks, SUVs, and minivans. Therefore, if you are using a sedan or sports car to get to your campouts, using a trailer hitch basket might require you first to get a trailer hitch installed on your vehicle. Since a trailer hitch does take away from the beauty of many cars—especially higher-end ones with sleek elegant lines—this might not be the route for everyone.

Most of these baskets come as a kit that will take you less than an hour to put together. Therefore, it is not something you want to buy the day of your campout unless you want to unnecessarily stress yourself out or arrive at camp well after dark. You will also need to get yourself a lockable trailer hitch pin so that you do not have to worry about someone stealing your basket when it is on your vehicle. It would not be a good way to start your weekend by having someone take your fully loaded basket when you stopped for dinner on the way to the campout.

Some have a tilt mechanism that allows it to be folded up once you get to camp. Since you are most likely not used to having it on your car and also because when it is fully unloaded it absolutely does not show in your rearview and side-view mirrors, there is a realistic chance of backing into things with it.

Many have a tight matrix of metal at the bottom, while others have sparsely spaced rods (that can lead to smaller objects falling out between them during transit). Some can have the ability to accommodate a large waterproof zippered bag that will directly connect to the basket. These bags are secured to the tray from below, using attached packing-style straps. This is an easy option for those that lack the skills or desire to use ratcheting straps to lock their gear into place. You just unzip it and start filling it up with smaller items like tripod chairs. You should find one that you believe is truly waterproof though. I have heard horror stories where someone purchased a "waterproof" one, to later find out (when their belongings were soaking wet) that that claim was not true. The only real downside to this zippered bag is that if you decide to haul something different or something that will push the limits of the bag, you will need to take the time to uninstall it.

As a final note, you can typically find both trailer hitch baskets and accessories (such as the locking pin and zippered bag) at travel rental stores (such as U-Haul) or tool stores. Take a look at the TheKeenCamper.com website for my current recommendations for products and retailers.

Roof cargo carriers can help provide more space

Another option that we use to add some additional cargo space, in addition to using a trailer hitch basket, is to use a rooftop cargo carrier. Depending on how much gear we need to haul, we sometimes will use one of them but will often take both the roof carrier and the trailer hitch basket if all seven of us are camping. Unlike the trailer hitch basket where there are not too many different styles (and you can't go too wrong with any of them), you do need to investigate and research which rooftop carrier is best for you. Some are designed to fit certain styles of cars, some are hard shell vs soft shell, and some are heavy and difficult to install without an entire crew helping you. The specific one I have is well-designed and can open from either side. This feature comes in handy when we get somewhere, and we need to unload from one specific side of our vehicle (due to space constraint such as a car being parked very close to us). On an unrelated note, you will need to be keenly aware of how tall your car is with the carrier installed—especially when considering parking in a parking garage that has a low clearance.

Fortunately, there are many online reviews you can use to help you make the best purchase. Make sure to consider whether it is waterproof and to look for online reviews that indicate this is indeed the case as well.

You will also need to consider how you are going to store this carrier when not in use. After letting mine sit on the floor of my garage (taking up lots of space) for a couple of years, I finally installed a ceiling-mounted hoist. This has not only helped declutter my garage but has also minimized any unnecessary wear and tear to the carrier. And on a side note, this carrier has provided a great place for us to store Christmas and birthday presents. Hopefully, my kids do not read this book!

Regarding what to pack in your car carrier, I like to put long things that would take up way too much space in my vehicle. With that said, these carriers do have weight limits. So, please know what that limit is and be conscientious of it. Back to the actual packing—I put all of the folding camp chairs and all of our rolled-up sleeping pads in there since they tend to be fairly wide, which results in them being long when rolled up. Sleeping bags can often be shoved in there as well.

Also, make sure your carrier is locked before you head out. I like the style of mine where the key cannot be removed from the lock unless the carrier is closed and locked. By putting the car carrier key on my main key ring, I cannot drive away unless the carrier is closed and has been locked. A friend of mine told me that one time he was traveling down the road and saw out the rearview mirror several board games flying around. He then realized they were his games and that he had forgotten to lock his car carrier before he pulled out. He never did that again!

When traveling to and from a campout, my goal is to be able to see through the length of the car and out the back window via the rearview mirror. Also, I want the aisle between the second-row captain's chairs to be clear as well. Satisfying both conditions makes me feel better about the entire packing and camping situation. It certainly helps me to feel that things are less out of control. Therefore, the trailer hitch basket and the rooftop car carrier greatly help us to stay more organized—and for me to be less stressed.

One last point concerns a hidden cost of these carriers. While most SUVs and minivans might have rails on the top of them, they might not have come with the crossbars that rooftop carriers need to attach to. If you are missing these crossbars, I would suggest getting the official ones for your make and model of car from your local dealership. It is not worth your rooftop carrier coming off while you are driving and possibly hurting others (and destroying your camping gear).

Cargo/trunk liners will keep your car interior from getting dirty

Obviously, camping is done outside, and the outside is not the cleanest. While we want our families to have the absolute best time they can (and not have to tiptoe around trying not to get things too dirty), we also do not want to be burdened with a lot of cleaning when we get home. And while I stand by the mantra of "do not bring things on a campout that will cause you to be upset if they come back dirty, ruined, or not at all," that is, of course, not the situation with our cars.

When we return home, we do not want permanent memories of the weekend campout via ground-in mud and dirt in the carpet and floor mats of our car. And, yes, people can take off their shoes when they get in the car which should help some. But remember that everything that was not exclusively inside the tent or up off the ground during the entire campout probably touched something dirty. Therefore, most everything will have some level of dirt on the bottom of it. From camp chair legs, to ice chests, to things that were set on the ground before being loaded into the tent or the car. Then, add in the factor of a little bit of rain or Sunday-morning condensation, and suddenly, this small amount of dirt becomes an even bigger issue in the form of mud.

One option that is reasonably affordable is the use of cargo, trunk, and floorboard liners. These are molded rubber trays that fit in these respective areas with approximately 3-inch vertical lips around their perimeters. These liners can be purchased directly from local car dealerships or online. All that you need to do is to specify your vehicle's make, model, year, and interior color to get liners that will perfectly fit your car and match the interior. I do not use these in the floorboard/mat areas but do use one in the cargo hold full time. I did have to make the judgment to buy one for the area for when the third-row seat is up. I could have purchased one for the configuration for when the third-row seat was out of the car, though. That would have provided maximum protection for my car, but it would have required me to store it (via keeping it rolled up) when I had the third-row seats installed.

This cargo liner has allowed me to be much more carefree on campouts and when returning from other outside activities. It has even worked well when we have needed to put wet grocery store bags, muddy bikes, dirty wagons, campfire logs, mulch, and even sod in the back of our vehicle. I chose not to get one for the floor mat areas because I didn't like the feel of the rubber under the heel of my foot. But many people who work outside in construction and on farms use these full-time.

The primary point of this section is to get organized for success so you can be more carefree—I want you to have fun on the campout and not fret about dirt in your car. I want you to enjoy this special time with your friends and family. The last thing I want you to do is to think about the interior of your vehicle getting ruined.

Avoid using backpacks unless you are backpacking

Backpacks are perfect for backpacking. For everyday camping, they can be extremely challenging. The reason is that packs are designed to carry the most amount of gear on your back in the most efficient manner. And while many backpacks have lots of zippered pockets and special side and bottom access panels, unless you are skilled and experienced with packing a backpack, you are going to find yourself taking everything out of your backpack every time you need to get to something. Based on my experience with this, this will grate on your nerves if you are on a regular family campout. When backpacking, it's easier to deal with this fact since there really are not other viable options. But by the end of your family campout, you will say *never again*! As a side note, unloading everything from your backpack is especially tough if you try to do so in the dark. Even with a headlamp, it can be challenging.

The better option for family campouts is to use duffle bags. I suggest buying all your family members the same exact style of duffle bag. Different colors for each person, colored ribbons tied to the handles, or even embroidered with their names will help everyone tell whose is whose. The benefit of the duffle bag is that when unzipped, you can easily see everything that is in them with one glance and not have to resort to digging through your gear. Additionally, being soft-sided, they are much easier to pack and shove into available spaces in your vehicle and your rooftop carrier. Backpacks with hard rigid frames and suitcases are very inefficient for packing in vehicles. While a traditional suitcase might be the best for an individual camper, it is the least desirable for the person packing the vehicle since they tend to create dead space around them (since the suitcases themselves cannot be compressed into a smaller volume).

A style of duffle bag that works well for us was designed to be a soft-sided camouflage ice chest. From the outside, it looks like a squared-off duffle bag with all the typical zippered pockets and straps. But on the inside, it is lined with a waterproof surface and has an exclusive access opening at the top meant for quickly grabbing a water bottle or soda.

Nest items together to save space

Recently, a friend and I attended a large Boy Scout event and met some other adult leaders that were cooking a turkey in a barrel. It was a great idea and very unique, but we both looked at each other and mentioned the challenge of hauling a 25-gallon barrel to and from campouts. We then talked to one of the cooks who suggested we could use a large galvanized steel trash can, but that still left the dilemma of how to deal with the space this monstrosity would take up in a vehicle. Later, as I thought about how I could make this work for our Boy Scout troop, I realized that the diameter of the trash can was probably wide enough (but not too wide) to hold stacked Dutch ovens.

This was especially interesting because whenever I use Dutch ovens for family camping, I already practice the concept of nesting. As a reminder, nesting is the art of stacking items inside one another. Think of the Russian nesting dolls you sometimes see. Regarding Dutch ovens, all of the non-refrigerated items for a dessert will fit inside a deep-version 12-inch wide Dutch oven. You can easily fit a boxed cake mix and three cans of pie filling inside one. If I have any dry mixes that I mixed up ahead of time for a cobbler or even corn bread, I will often put those inside an empty Dutch oven as well. As is discussed in the Dutch Oven chapter in *The Keen Camper Camping with Kids Volume 2* book, after each Dutch oven is used, I typically coat my cleaned cast-iron items with coconut oil. But, where do I store that oil? My solution is to keep a plastic jar of coconut oil in one of my Dutch ovens.

Regarding KP, I nest three washtubs by stacking them together. When

driving to the campsite, I usually put dry goods in the very top tub that will later be used in the recipes for some of our meals early on in the campout. And, yes, I do need to deal with these temporarily placed items when I get to the campsite and want to use these tubs to do KP. But for getting to camp, this is an easy approach for saving space. Speaking of KP, I usually bring a 24-quart aluminum pot to heat water in. On the way to the campout, I keep my drip bags, dish soap, and bleach in this pot as well.

While some nesting opportunities are obvious—like stacking washtubs and hog pans (for Dutch oven charcoal cooking)—you will need to be on the lookout for the rest of them. But like with anything else, as you camp more, you will get better and better at this.

Packing odd–shaped and dirty charcoal–cooking accessories

Some camping gear just does not pack very well. One of the most challenging for me is my charcoal chimneys. Except for when they were brand new and unused, they are dirty, sometimes rusted, and tend to clang against things around them in the car. Part of the clanging issues is my own doing since I like to put the chimney in the top hog pan with the lid lifter and charcoal tongs lying next to it. What I usually end up doing is to place the chimney inside a large black garbage bag, and then place it in the hog pan on its side. For the times I take two chimneys, I have been known to put them next to each other to save space—knowing very well they will probably clang against each other on the trip out to the campout. Oh well, everything is a tradeoff.

The best option that I have seen is a fold-up charcoal chimney. Unfortunately, full-size versions might not be available anymore except the secondary markets like eBay and Craigslist. It is made of stainless steel, folds up, and slips into a very nice and rugged flat sleeve/case. If you can find one, jump on it. As I have mentioned, you need to be very careful about putting any items in black garbage bags due to (1) trash getting thrown in the bag with it, or (2) the bag and the chimney getting thrown away if mistaken for trash.

For the charcoal tongs, I usually take a zip tie and create a muzzle that can be slid over them to keep them closed during transport. For both the tongs and lid lifter, I often wrap them in a towel to:

☀ Keep my car and other gear they might touch clean.

- ☀ Keep them from cutting/damaging my car's interior.
- ☀ To keep them from clanging together.

The bottom line is that charcoal accessories are challenging to transport. Just take a big, deep breath and do your best. Over time, you will find what works best for you. And as always, you can share your thoughts, successes, and struggles with other campers on the TheKeenCamper.com website.

Leaving critical gear at home
when you run out of space is not the best idea

Do not do it! I could just end this paragraph right now, but instead, I will walk you through a few personal stories about why *not* to do this.

Because of being poorly organized a few times, I have run into a bind on Friday afternoons while packing for a weekend campout. As the time continues to fly by, the impending sunset is inching closer, and the car is already so full that it might not even be safe for my kids to ride in it. So, occasionally I have made the mistake of "cutting my losses" and just leaving items behind—so that we can get going. This has been due to various reasons some of which include:

- ☀ I can't be bothered.
- ☀ We just need to leave.
- ☀ The car is just too full already.
- ☀ I do not want to take a second car.
- ☀ I do not want to pull things out and repack.
- ☀ The feeling that we are bringing way too many items.

Every time I have made the judgment to leave items at home because they were not yet packed, I have regretted it.

On one campout, I decided I could not be bothered to bring snacks. I tend to not snack in general and can easily not snack on campouts as well, but that is not the case for my family. While I am sure they could get used to not snacking, not giving them any warning or say-so and expecting them to immediately adjust and adapt lead to a lot of whining—especially since other families we were camping with did bring snacks, juice bags/boxes, etc.

Another mistake I made one time (due to a lack of space) was to not bring a chair for everyone in my family. I guess I somehow thought my youngest child would not care or that she could share a chair with someone else. The lack of a chair for everyone reared its not-so-pretty head first thing Saturday morning during breakfast when *I* did not have a place to sit to drink my coffee and eat my breakfast. Since there was not a picnic table at this campsite, it was either the chairs we brought or nothing. This lack continued for the remaining meals and even at the Saturday night campfire. Since I was a chair short, and it was my decision to not bring enough chairs, it was only appropriate that I not have one.

I have also not brought my propane lantern. While many families are used to not having a great light source, once you become accustomed to one, it is hard to adjust and not feel a great sense of lack and inconvenience when you do not have a propane lantern.

Another time, I decided to not bring my sleeping pad and decided to bring an exercise mat instead. That was one of the worst night's sleep I ever had.

The list goes on and on. Not bringing ingredients for dessert because you thought you had already spent enough money on campout food. Not bringing coffee because you didn't want to round up all of the mugs for all of the coffee drinkers in the family. Not bringing the already-paid-for canopy. Not bringing the sand toys. Not bringing Uno . . .

Do not do it. If you and your family are used to bringing certain things, then bring them. Even if it causes you to arrive later than you wanted to or to be a little (or a lot) more crowded in the car than you wanted. And to help you with the temptation to cut corners, start your packing process early as described earlier in this chapter.

When should you consider bringing two cars?

The simple answer to this question is . . . it depends. If taking multiple vehicles to the campout will allow your family to have the best time possible, then it is worth the small amount of extra gas (compared to the great memories you will be creating together). There are two main reasons that I have seen for needing to bring two cars to a campout for a family. The first is when you honestly just have more gear that you have space for. With five kids, our

family of seven used to need to bring two cars. But since buying a trailer hitch basket and rooftop car carrier, we no longer need to do this. In fact, on a few campouts, we had a reasonable amount of spare room and I could easily see out the rear window. With this said, we sometimes need to put the canopy box (that is 5x1x1-feet) between the two captain's chairs and up on the top of the middle section of the third-row seat when traveling to the campout. So, even when things are manageable, they are still not always perfect.

The other reason is when one or more people in your family have schedule conflicts that are going to prevent them from being able to camp the entire weekend. On a recent Cub Scout family campout, the primary person leading the campout wanted to arrive at the state park soon after they opened Friday morning to get the best campsites available for our group of 20+ families. She then wanted to enjoy the rest of the day with a hike and lunch with her two children. However, her husband worked in downtown Dallas and was not going to be able to leave until Friday evening. While I know they would have preferred to drive together to and from the campground, they knew it just was not in the cards; they just accepted that fact, made the decision to drive two cars, and moved on.

I have also seen a need for this when someone can only stay one night or needs to leave early on Sunday morning. While it would be great if everyone could put their life and other priorities on hold to go camping, I understand that this is not always possible or reasonable to do. Therefore, you need to do what is best for your family. What does not work well is when you have individuals on a Boy Scout campout that leave early. This has the side effect of requiring everyone else to clean up and pack the shared equipment for them. But for a family campout, having one of the parents or older children depart early is manageable since the rest of the family can just pitch in a little (or a lot) more.

One caveat to all of this for those that want to arrive late and leave early . . . It can be a distracting situation for everyone else who is already enjoying being in the "campout groove." Therefore, please be mindful of this. If you arrive late or need to leave early, while being up front with your fellow campers, try to come and go discreetly.

Adjust your packing list based on where and when you are going

Configurable packing lists are a must-have. Otherwise, you have a high probability to under-pack or over-pack. One of the worst things is to arrive somewhere and realize that you cannot take advantage of a key feature or activity because you are not prepared. An example would be that you arrive at the campout not knowing that there were bike trails, and you did not bring a bike, or you brought a pathway bike, only to find there were only mountain bike trails. Still, it would be worse to take the time to pack a bike and then find out there were no trails at all. The examples are endless. Let's examine a few of them.

Summer
        Sunscreen, Artic mist coolers, bug spray

Water & Summer
        Swimsuits, beach towels

Sand Volleyball Court or Beachfront
        Sand toys

Mountain Bike Trail
        Mountain bike, helmet

Showers
        Towel, shampoo, conditioner, washcloth, body wash

Hiking Trails
>   Day pack, hiking shoes

White-water Rafting, Canoeing, Paddleboats
>   Hat, water shoes

Boat on a Large Lake or Ocean
>   Dramamine, scopolamine patch, motion sickness bracelet

Cold Weather
>   Full sleeping bag, fleece blanket or liner, ski cap

Hot Weather
>   Sleeping bag liner

I think that you get the point. You need to have mini-checklists based on the type of campout you are planning. Please take a look at my **CLEAN Packing** checklist at the TheKeenCamper.com. While you can get more details on the website, the **CLEAN Packing** system utilizes the key parameters of your campout to create a custom packing list just for you.

C = Climate

L = Length

E = Environment

A = Activity

N = Necessities

Bring small grocery store–style plastic bags for dirty shoes

Camping, by its very nature, is dirty. Also, to quote something I like from those that practice Leave No Trace: When you camp, you only want to "take" pictures and leave behind "footprints." With that said, you do not want to take home memories such as stained floor mats and stained car

interiors. So, while it is a very small item and probably not worth an entire section, make sure to bring a plastic grocery store bag for each shoe (*not* each pair of shoes) that you bring on the campout. If you bring five people who each bring two pairs of shoes, you should bring 20 grocery-style bags. And per the nesting guidance given earlier, just stuff all of them into one single bag. While probably not the safest thing to do, I have been on some campouts where I drove home wearing only socks (or barefoot) and no shoes due to it raining at the last minute and my shoes were covered in mud.

Use large garbage bags for wet items when you pack up to head home

In each of our duffle bags, I usually put two to three large (33 gallons or larger) black garbage bags that are folded into a very compact footprint. These are for unexpected events. We primarily use these bags for wet or damp items. More often than not, it is not rain that we find ourselves up against; instead, it is heavy condensation that we find covering everything on the last day of our campout. While I know that if we waited a few hours, it would most definitely evaporate, usually I am wanting to make progress on getting home. Sometimes I will take the rainfly and find somewhere to hang it up while I pack up the rest of the tent. If not, I will take each fabric part of the tent and place it in its dedicated black garbage back. If everything is wet, you can probably put them all in one bag. But if the bottom of your tent is muddy and the rainfly is just wet, you probably want to put them in separate bags. This is done to reduce the number of cross contamination messes that are created. Mud on the bottom of a tent or tarp is OK. Mud smashed into the mesh of a tent is not.

You have to be careful with this approach, however. Once we went camping with a group of Boy Scouts to a spring camporee. The weather was fantastic and dry all weekend—that is until we started to pack up and it started raining. Most of our tents got wet, and we put some of them in black garbage bags. As with most Boy Scout campouts, we put our gear in the troop's trailer. Because it was raining when we returned to the meeting and pickup location, we only pulled our personal gear off the troop trailer and agreed to unload the remainder of the trailer at our meeting which was scheduled for two days later on Tuesday. That Tuesday night, as we unpacked the trailer, we put wet trash that was mixed in with our troop gear into a black garbage bag next to the trailer. Nobody wondered where this bag came from. And I just assumed that someone had gotten it out of the box of garbage bags we carry with us on the trailer. Well, for some reason, something told me to look in the bag. And what I found was a blue tent and an assortment of tent poles—along with a lot of trash that had just been put in there. It turned out that this was one of the black garbage bags that we had thrown a wet tent into a few days earlier. After removing the nasty trash, we were able to isolate the tent and sent it home with its 13-year-old owner. Everything ended up working out fine, but it was a close call. Fortunately, it was an inexpensive tent, but what if it had been an expensive one? My point is to be mindful that there is always a risk when putting items in a "trash" bag that it could be mistaken as trash.

What lessons in leading your family can you take away from this aspect of camping?

"Stick to the Plan"

At the end of the chapter on "Tents & Shelters," I discussed the concept of "Expect the Expected" and how it was applicable outside of the domain of camping. This chapter's real theme is a sister topic which I call "Stick to the Plan." Once you have a good understanding of what makes a great campout for your family and have put together a plan to make it happen each time, you need to stick to it.

In both my personal and work life, I have experienced and witnessed many failures or shortcomings due to someone (including myself) not staying with the plan of record. Imagine concluding that you are not living a healthy lifestyle and you decide to visit your family doctor, who, in turn, tells you that you have high blood pressure and need to take medication daily to control it. The doctor then calls in a prescription on your behalf, your medical insurance pays for most of it, you pick it up, and then you take it home. You take it faithfully every day, but for some reason, you determine it is a pain to get it out of the medicine cabinet and take it because you are stressed out trying to get out of the house, take your kids to school, and get to the office on time. You then selfishly convince yourself it is OK and that it does not impact anyone but you.

One night, you find yourself at the ER due to your blood pressure being off the charts. You must explain to your family how it was your fault that they had to all step out of the play one of your kids was in to go to the ER with you.

Do not get me wrong. I know that we are not perfect. I am not perfect, and neither are you. But once you have taken the time to put together a plan and have everything lined up to be successful . . . just do it. Stick to the plan!

How many people do you know that determined how to beat an addiction, only to fall victim to it again because they did not stick to the plan? The alcoholic who went into a bar or liquor store. The gambling addict who went to a trade show in Las Vegas with his coworkers.

Beyond the personal damage that you do to yourself, think of the damage that you do to those around you. Your kids and spouse are counting on you to be successful and are looking for a role model for what success looks like. The only suggestion that I have for you is to focus on your objectives. If your objective is for your family to have the best family campout, camp a few times, determine what works best for your family, develop a plan for future campouts, and then stick to that plan. If your goal is to be a better spouse or parent, observe what is working and what is not, put together a plan to keep the good things going, and try different things when things are not going the best. And then . . . *Stick to the Plan.*

My final comment is that it is really tough for some people to stick to the plan. If you are one of those people, ask someone who cares about you to be your accountability partner. Once you do (and they say yes), your chance of being successful will improve greatly.

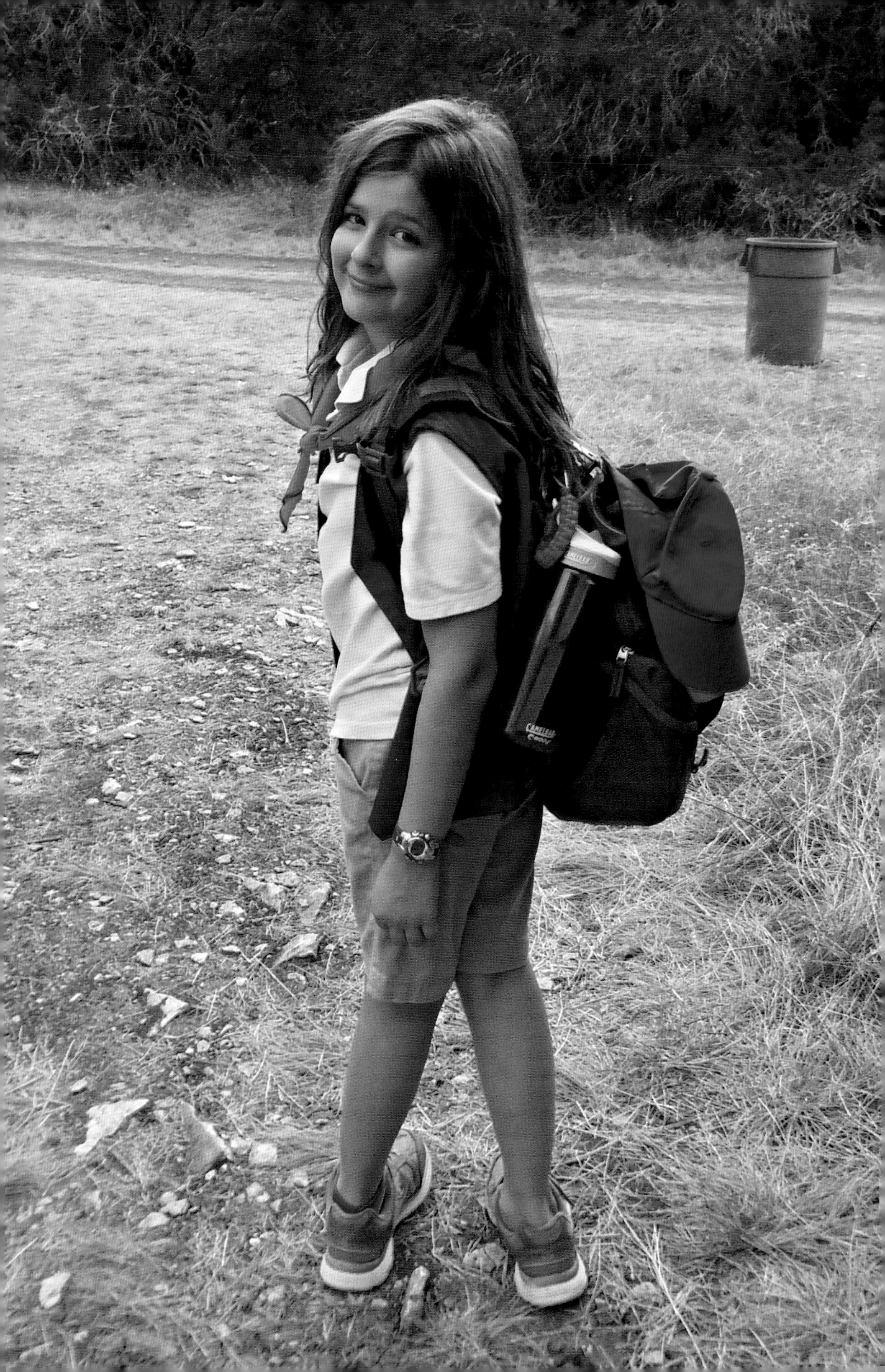

CHAPTER 6

CONSERVATION MINDED

Being conservation minded can lead to a more natural campout experience

Being conservation minded can add an additional level of uniqueness to your family campout. If you do everything the same way you would at home, what is the point of camping? And to be conservation minded, you do not necessarily need to have the mind-set of a doomsday prepper or survivalist. A big point about being conservation minded is that while you are in the peaceful and natural outdoors, try to really get in touch with that naturalness. As we get started on this chapter, take the subject of trash. At home, I do not give much thought to the waste we generate. We create it, we separate it (into what is recyclable and what is not), and then it gets taken away. If you have not done so before, take a minute to realize how much trash you generate on a campout. It is truly staggering. From a personal perspective, the less trash my family produces on a campout, the closer I feel to nature. Even though we work diligently to keep our campsite picked up and litter free, the mere act of even seeing this trash around the campsite makes me realize how far from nature my life has drifted.

Use refillable water bottles

Nothing tends to take away from the complete outdoor experience more than generating litter at and around your campsite. And when I say litter,

I am talking about the food-related packaging items you brought that tend to spread like a wildfire—sitting on various ledges, tables, and chairs around your campsite. The biggest offender usually being single-use disposable water bottles. I have camped with people that reach for a brand-new unopened water bottle every time they are thirsty. They even open new ones because their partially

consumed present one is no longer cold. And more times than not, they leave the partially consumed ones resting wherever they were last placed. Even with a typical-size family, seeing 10 or more water bottles sitting around one's campsite is not uncommon. When drinking sports and fruit drinks, the situation tends to be even worse since people are even less inclined to consume these types of drinks once they heat up to room temperature.

When we first started camping as a family, my preference was to bring an orange construction site style cooler, load it up with tap water, and have everyone fill up refillable water bottles from it. Over the years as I have learned more about public tap water, I am less inclined to ask others to do this. And because the taste of local tap water can vary from location to location, my family tended to drink less water than normal (although they needed to consume more), because they did not enjoy the taste. Lately, I have been bringing several 2-gallon containers of filtered spring water that have a built-in closeable spout. This way, everyone gets to enjoy the great-tasting water they drink at home, and you completely get away from needing to purchase, bring, and use individual disposable water bottles.

As a final note, if you choose to go the route of bringing single-use disposable water bottles, please bring a permanent felt tip marker that can be used to mark people's initial(s) on the cap. This allows everyone to keep track of which bottle belongs to them while they are being consumed. Also, because pens and markers tend to grow legs and walk away, it might be a good idea to attach the marker to a secure object (like a picnic table) with a string.

Paper products generate the largest amount of trash on a campout

With large groups, it is easier to utilize disposable plates, cups, napkins, and silverware. This is especially true if you are hosting a single-meal event such as a cookout, picnic, or just a dinner at your house. Unless you have a tremendous amount of free time, it would be crazy to use items that needed to be washed, dried, and put away for a large number of people for a single meal. But for your family campouts (where you are just feeding your family and feeding them approximately five meals across the entire weekend), it makes more sense to use mess kits and to not use any disposable cups, plates, or silverware. The only disposable items you should consider using (and do need to bring) are napkins, paper towels, and antibacterial or alcohol-based wipes. Regarding napkins, to keep things as simple as possible, I would suggest using select-a-size paper towels (that rip off in half-size rectangular sections versus full-size square sections). These can also be used as the official paper towels (to sanitize your work surfaces) as well.

To go with this approach, you will need to have a mess kit (or the equivalent of a mess kit) for every one of your campers. A complete mess kit includes a plate, bowl, cup, mug, knife, fork, spoon, and a mesh drip bag. As always, to save space and money, you can get away with a single plate (versus a plate and bowl). You can also get away with a mug (hopefully insulated) instead of having both a cup and a mug. Also available are three-in-one cutlery items that have a spoon/fork (spork) at one end and a knife-like edge somewhere on the end opposite the part you grip. These will enable you to reduce your silverware items from three per person to one.

When my son and I camp with other boys and dads, we each take our mess kit items in separate mesh bags—one for me and one for my son. When we do family camping, we separate the items by type (plate, bowl, mug) instead of separating them by owner. Although we have multiple sets of different-colored mess kits (so that we can easily keep track of which ones are ours) when camping with groups, we have sometimes had trouble keeping track of which ones are ours since so many people bring the same styles and colors of mess kits. Therefore, we now write our last name on the backside

of every piece of our mess kit. And I mean EVERYTHING—even, the knife, spoon, and fork. Also, make sure to only write your last name on items. This way, any of your family members can use any of these items when camping on their own without the family. I have seen that kids especially do not like to use items that have their siblings' names on them.

If you do use mess kits instead of paper products, you will greatly reduce the level of trash you generate. Otherwise, your garbage bag will be overflowing within the first 24 hours. This might be hard to grasp, but imagine a family of five needing five plates, five sets of silverware, and five cups for every meal. This adds up to needing 25 place settings for the entire campout! That is a lot of potential paper products and trash. And while we buy and transport these items neatly stacked and nested, we typically end up disposing of them individually, which is very space inefficient—thus filling up your garbage bag very, very quickly.

A final comment on mess kits. While sometimes hard to find, there is a great divided tray by Eagle brand mugs that is wonderful for your little ones. Since we eat most of our meals sitting in chairs, it can be difficult for our little ones to balance their plate and cup (which does not always fit in the chair's cup holder due to its handle). The Eagle brand tray is hard like a school lunchroom tray. Additionally, it has dividers for different types of foods, and best of all it has a circular area for placing your Eagle brand mug with a special slit for the handle to fit through. It is very cool.

Environmentally friendly dish soap should be used on campouts

Hopefully, we all want the places we camp to be beautiful and to look very natural. With that said, it would be best to only have the normal native plants and trees (that were intended) to be there. The native vegetation is there at these specific spots for a reason—because they can thrive with the natural baseline level of water, nutrients, and sunlight at those specific areas. These plants do not respond well to the pollutants we bring with us to our campsites. While it might not seem like it, dish soap is one of these pollutants.

While your grandmother's dish soap was most likely safe for the environment, many of the dish soaps that are available today are petroleum based and contain scents to make them smell better. My concern is how do the chemicals in our dish soap impact the campsites when we dump our dirty dishwater that is full of petroleum-based products and scents into the woods? While your one-time dumping will most likely not make a significant impact, these campsites are used year-round and year after year. Therefore, everyone's collective impact could be significant. When we camp, one of our goals is to depart Sunday morning feeling like we partnered with "Mother Nature" to use the campgrounds but not abuse the campgrounds.

So, you might be thinking, *"OK, we will just pour our dirty dishwater down a drain."* First, there are not usually sewage drains on the campouts, and even if there were, you should not dump anything in them that might be harmful to the environment since most feed into nearby ponds, lakes, or streams. Also, since many of the bathroom drains feed into septic systems, you need to be conscientious of what you put in them as well.

The alternative that addresses all of this is to use environmentally safe dish soap. While it used to be difficult to find this type of dish soap except in very small containers at specialty camping supply stores, you can now readily find several varieties in standard-size bottles that are "good enough" at most grocery stores.

Assuming that your dishwater is reasonably safe for the environment, the next thing to focus on is how you dispose of it. First, move out approximately 10 feet into the woods from the perimeter of your campsite. Next, do not dump out the water in one big splash. Instead, scoop it out with a cup or mug, and then disperse it across a reasonably-sized area from where you are standing. Be mindful that you do not pour it in places that will drain back into your campsite—thus, making your campsite muddy and getting the bottom of your tent wet.

As a last note, the scents and fragrances used in many of today's non-environmentally safe soaps tend to attract wild animals. And while most of us like animals, we do not want them to show up uninvited to our campsites due to the type of dish soap we used.

What KP equipment do you need and does it matter what you get?

One of my guiding premises is that smart people learn from their mistakes, and wise people learn from the mistakes of others. With that said, I have a trusted friend who is both a camping gear junkie and was the Scoutmaster for a sizeable Boy Scout troop. After several iterations, he finally came to what I believe is the absolute best KP setup I have seen.

He uses three washtubs from Rubbermaid. They are thick, sturdy, and measure roughly 21x17x7 inches and are listed as having a 7.6-gallon capacity. While I have typically purchased them at restaurant supply stores, I have recently seen them at wholesalers like Sam's Club. Just like with the Dutch oven "oil" pans (that I discuss in the Dutch oven chapter in *The Keen Camper Camping With Kids Volume 2*) that are actually hog pans, these are not called washtubs. Instead, they are officially known as "bus trays" and are used in the restaurant industry. For those not familiar with the behind-the-scenes workings of a restaurant, bus boys are the individuals that clear off the tables after you are done eating. These bus trays are intended to carry a good amount of weight, including liquid, and will not flex under a load. To make things easy, label both short ends with a permanent maker with what that tub will be used for and what solution will go in it. These markings are: "Wash—Hot Water with Soap," "Sanitize—Hot Water with Bleach," and "Rinse—Cold Water."

Now, let's get to why these are the best tubs. First, they are super strong and are practically unbreakable. I suspect that if you ran over them with your car they would break, but that is probably outside the scope of the typical wear and tear that would happen on a campout. I have seen people try to use smaller and less industrial wash basins with poor results—they tend to crack easily, show stress marks, and can flex when loaded with water. While you will most likely only transport these tubs full of water when you are filling them or when you get ready to dump them out after use, that load can be enough to damage them and possibly cause you to spill water on yourself.

The second reason is that that they are essentially inert or neutral. Thus, using them with water, soap, bleach, and dirty food grime will not add any wear and tear to them. I have seen people use galvanized steel buckets, but they will react with the water and can rust. When I wash dishes in my recommended bus tubs, I come away feeling they are clean. When I am forced to use someone else's  galvanized steel ones, I do not. In fact, I tend to think the dishes—while looking clean—are not.

Last, these bins are huge and can accommodate almost every piece of cookware, bowl, knife, and even grill grates (used for grilling hamburgers) that you might need to clean on a campout. With a typical metal bucket or small washtub, it is hard to fit much in them. And since items tend to not fully fit in them, it is very difficult to focus on cleaning the item when 90 percent of it is hanging over the edge. Also, it is nearly impossible to do the final bleach dip effectively when you need to rotate the item several times to get it complete dipped—if you can even do it at all. And in the worst case, the tub can even topple over if too much of a heavy item being washed is hanging over the edge.

Finally, by using the same style tub for all three steps, you will be able to stack/ nest them. This, in turn, will help minimize their footprint in your vehicle on the way to and from the campout. Also, back to my earlier discussion on nesting in the "Checklists, Packing & Getting There" chapter, I always fill the top tub with items that need to be transported to the campout but that can be removed once we get there.

The steps in the KP process need to be followed

The process of the KP system that I recommend is a slight modification of the First Class rank requirements in the *Boy Scout Handbook*. It is also known as the three-bucket system. The first bucket is for Washing and is sometimes labeled with a "W." The second is for Sanitation and is sometimes labeled with an "S." And finally, the third bucket is for Rinsing and is sometimes labeled "R."

The first step is to wipe every single bit of food from your dishes using toilet paper. I recommend buying the absolute cheapest, single-ply toilet tissue you can find. I also recommend people use just one square of toilet tissue at a time and not use a wad of it. If this step is not done correctly and thoroughly, the first and subsequent tubs will quickly become unsanitary.

A quick story . . . I was on a campout where we had taken a good amount of time to get the KP station set up, including having heated the water for the Wash and Sanitation tubs. During a short timeframe when many of us were not paying close attention to the KP line, a new dad (that had not camped with our Boy Scout troop before) came up to the first tub with all his uneaten food still on his plate and dropped it in. This first tub was now completely unusable. Needless to say, nobody behind him was thrilled with us having to completely dump out that water, clean out the tub, and reheat another batch of water for that tub (plus the Sanitation tub which would have been cold by the time the new wash water was ready). Therefore, whenever my family camps with families that we have not camped with before, I usually ask one of my kids to stand guard at the KP station. It is amusing seeing one my little ones inform grown adults that they need to get all their food off their plates, and then must send them back to the toilet paper stage when they have done a half-baked job.

The Wash Tub

This tub is filled with very warm water. It should not be so hot that you cannot immerse your hands without being in pain. This tub should have a reasonable amount of environmentally friendly liquid dish soap so that there is a fair amount of suds. You should also add several sponges and dish brushes. The purpose of this tub is to get the dishes clean and to remove any remnants of food that were not removed by the toilet tissue wiping. By the end of doing KP, this tub should only be slightly discolored (gray) and should not feel or look unsanitary.

The Sanitation Tub

This tub is the same temperature as the washtub. Additionally, you will need to add one capful of regular standard bleach to this water. The purpose of this step is to kill or neutralize any bacteria that might still be on your dishes. Another option is to add a bleach tablet. This alternative has the advantage of minimizing the hazards associated with using and storing liquid bleach.

The Rinse Tub

This tub is filled with the same amount of water as the other two tubs, but it should be normal room "cold" faucet temperature. Additionally, this tub does not need any sponges or brushes either. The purpose of this tub is to rinse the soap and bleach off the dishes. As a side note, if you do not get the soap from the first step off the dishes, you could end up with a thin film of soap being left on your dishes. The first problem with this is that the next time you use these dishes, there might be a detectable soap aftertaste associated with the meals. The second issue is that ingesting soap (even a small amount that is undetectable to your taste buds) can lead to diarrhea. If the entire KP process is done correctly, this water should be fairly clear after having washed and rinsed all of the dishes.

As a side story, when my son's Boy Scout troop got a new trailer for hauling gear to campouts, we used it a few times before we added shelving to it. Unfortunately, on the way back from one of our weekend campouts, the container of liquid bleach fell on its side and ended up leaking out. The following month, we detected a strong bleach smell upon opening the trailer and found a 6x6-inch section of the plywood flooring in our new trailer had been eaten away by the bleach. After this experience, we looked for and found the better option of dissolvable bleach tablets.

Now, back to the sanitation tub. If the wash cleaning step was done correctly, this sanitation step is unnecessary. This is a failsafe step that is critically important when you have dishwashers that are less than perfect (such as very young children). As a side note, I do not let my younger children work with

the sanitation tub due to the bleach possibly injuring them or bleaching their clothes. I do let them get fully engaged in all the other steps. Once again, if the first "wash" KP step is done correctly, the sanitation tub should be perfectly clear—as though nobody even used it—when all of meal's KP has been completed.

On a side note, we did a practice "day campout" with my oldest daughter's American Heritage Girls troop. At that event, I showed a group of more than 20 girls and 20 adults how to do KP. While everyone absolutely loved it, I noticed afterward that one of the mother's navy-blue sweatshirt hoodie had gray cuffs after KP was finished. It turns out she did not get the 411 that there was a reasonable amount of bleach in the second tub, and that was the tub she was working at.

As you can surmise, if the above three-tub KP process is followed, you should significantly reduce the incidents of people getting sick on or after your campouts. Besides people not getting sick, you might also notice that while kids might not like doing the dishes at home, they tend to love doing KP on campouts!

Use a drip line to keep your washed dishes clean

The last step in the KP process involves the use of a drip line. The drip line is a rope tied between two objects (typically trees) where you can hang mesh drip bags that contain the dishes you just washed to "drip" dry.

Whenever you pull your dishes out of the Rinse (cold water) tub, you need to immediately do something with them. One option is to use a dish towel or paper towels to dry them off. Another option is to set them down somewhere to dry, and a third option (and my favorite) is to use a drip line.

I always recommend that people buy mess kits with a mesh bag. You can also buy a *beach toy* drip mesh bags as well for larger items. One modification that I suggest is using a carabiner in combination with these mesh bags to easily clip them on and off the drip line. Otherwise, you will have to tie the mesh bag's drawstring to the drip line. While that is not too difficult with an empty mesh bag, it can be challenging to untie when weighted down with dishes.

Regarding the drip line, I would suggest a one-quarter-inch diameter polypropylene (poly) rope. While the actual drip line should be approximately 10 feet, you will need additional rope to wrap around the trees and to tie the appropriate knots; therefore, you will need at least a 25-foot rope. Additionally, hanging this drip line will provide a great opportunity to improve your knot-tying skills. Your drip line is essentially going to be a clothesline. To hang a clothesline or drip line, you need to use two basic knots. First, tie a "two half hitches" knot around a tree and cinch it tight to the tree. Using the other end of the rope, tie it around a similarly sized tree (diameter wise) using a "taut line." Then, slide the "taut line" knot along the length of the rope (away from the tree it was tied around) to tighten the rope until it does not sag under the load of the mesh bags loaded with dishes.

And while it should not be your goal to "show off," I can attest that your kids, spouse, and others will be very impressed that you can properly hang a drip line. Knot too bad, is it?

Reduce trash at its source by being mindful of foods that have a lot of packaging

If you are using mess kits instead of paper products, the biggest source of your trash will be the packaging associated with your foods. This would include by meal:

Breakfast: egg carton, bacon/sausage packaging, orange juice bottle, milk bottle, and pancake shake mix/shaker/disposable container

Lunch: Potato chips and cookie packaging

Dinner: Cans, boxes, seasoning packages

Dessert: Pie filling cans, cake boxes, butter wrappers

If you wanted to go to the extreme, you could remove these items from their original packaging, transfer them to washable containers at home, and recycle the original packaging at home. I strongly suggest not doing this since it has some shortcomings. It wastes valuable time packing and cleaning up extra items on the campout. It also requires you to refrigerate more items (and thus, have a greater chance of getting sick if these items do not stay cold enough) such as pie filling and beans, which are fine in their unopened/sealed cans but once opened, need to be refrigerated.

The main point is to be *mindful* of the food items you bring and the trash that they potentially generate. If you can bring one milk jug and one orange juice bottle instead of individual ones, do it. If you can bring big bags of chips instead of individual ones, even better. I think you get the idea. Any effort to think through this ahead of the campout will help to reduce the amount of trash you ultimately must deal with on the campout itself.

Pack out the items that can be recycled

This is a tough one. The last thing that you want to do is to be feeling this great sense of satisfaction of communing with nature . . . just to realize that your carbon footprint increased during your campout. So, what is a carbon footprint? At its essence, it is the level at which your existence negatively impacts the environment and the earth.

Most parts of the United States have great recycling services these days where the bulk of your trash no longer goes to the landfill but instead, goes to a recycling center. But unfortunately, most state parks and campgrounds have one, and only one, type of trash dumpster—and all its contents are headed to a landfill. This leaves you with a few choices. One is to rinse, bag, and take your recyclables home and dispose of them more effectively. To this end, I have been known to set up two trash bags at the campsite—one for landfill trash and one to take home to recycle.

The second choice is to transfer the contents of certain items to containers that can be washed on the campout. The original packaging (which is hopefully recyclable) can be more properly dealt with at home before you leave. This concept was discussed in more detail in the previous section of this chapter.

I think this needs to be a judgment call for everyone. Here is one example. We use a Camp Chef Explorer stove with a half griddle that is designed with a "can" holder to collect grease. Therefore, I try to always use empty soup-style cans on campouts that fit that holder. Since I know I have an on-going need for cans to catch grease, I usually save the soup-size ones I use on campouts. I just rinse them and then drop them in the box for my stove for use on future campouts once they are dry. Since reuse is the best type of recycling, this grease catcher can idea is the type that I aggressively look for. What can *you* do to eliminate the need to throw so many recyclable items in the dumpster at the campground?

Another option is to consider working with your local campground or state park to set up a recycling service. As a service project, you could even raise money for a recycling dumpster and arrange for a service to start collecting it from the campground.

What trash can be burned?

The answer: very little. You need to be very careful and mindful of what items you want to consider burning on your campout via the campfire. The initial concern should be whether the item will be completely consumed by the fire. The secondary and probably the more important concern is the safety related to the fumes produced from burning the item.

At a recent American Heritage Girls Family Campout, we decided to perform a flag retirement ceremony after Saturday night's campfire. For a flag retirement ceremony, you cut the stripes of the flag into individual red and white strips. You then cut the blue section out as a separate section. By the way, some people will cut out the individual white stars. Some of the flags that we retired were 100 percent cotton, while others were made from a synthetic-blend. The great news is that both varieties of flags were quickly consumed by the fire. The bad news is that some nasty-smelling fumes were produced from the synthetic-blend ones. After the ceremony, several people wanted to use the fire for s'mores. But because of our concern over the synthetics and other petroleum-based products that were now part of the base of coals, we did not feel comfortable with making s'mores and told the girls, to their great disappointment, "no." Going forward, we started only retiring 100 percent cotton flags. If you do choose to retire synthetic-blend flags, please take some additional precautions. For example, do not stand close to the fire. By doing so, you will be able to minimize breathing in potentially harmful fumes.

So what can you burn (other than firewood)? I feel comfortable burning empty bags of charcoal. Other than that, we typically do not burn anything else in the fire other than wood and charcoal. And regarding wood, use real logs and not pieces of furniture and cabinetry you brought from home. Burning them can generate fumes from the painted and lacquered finishes. A general rule of thumb is to shoot for a campfire that smells natural and not chemical.

Here's another story. On a Cub Scout family campout, we had a dad that thought it would be neat to show off, so he put a sealed soda can and a sealed can of beans on a roaring fire. We struggled when this happened because we did not want to disrespect the father in front of the boys (and in front of his son who was watching on). What we ended up doing was to discreetly take him aside while someone took a shovel and quietly removed the items from the fire while nobody was looking. We were concerned because the physics and chemistry of the situation spelled danger everywhere. A closed container where the volume is going to expand under pressure as the contents heat up could result in an explosion with metal shrapnel. For the soda can, it is a little less dangerous since the pop top will probably give way or the can will melt before it explodes. That might not be the case for a steel bean can though. The bottom line is, do not ever put anything on or in the fire other than paper bags from the charcoal. And if it is easier to tell your kids *nothing* gets put on the fire, you can either throw the empty charcoal bag in the dumpster (where it will quickly disintegrate in the landfill) or you can pack it out to recycle it at home.

What lessons in leading your family can you take away from this aspect of camping?

"Lifestyle Trade-offs"

Just like the previous chapters, I looked for the underlying principle at work in this chapter that I could apply to my everyday life (and specifically while leading my family). It was obvious to me that it was our "Lifestyle Trade-offs." Since everyone has a fixed and limited amount of free time, money, and mental/emotional/physical capacity, your life is the grand total of all of the lifestyle trade-offs you have made. And because we are all individuals with different priorities and interests, the lifestyle choices we end up making are different from those made by others.

What has made me so successful in the area of family camping and helping others enjoy their family camping is to know what is important to me at any given time, and then make decisions (and trade-offs) based on that worldview. While I obviously prefer my worldview and the lenses that I choose to see the world through, the key to my success has not been due as much to my personal choices as it has been that "I made choices." And a key aspect of making these choices has been to truly accept that it is almost impossible to be the master of *many* without becoming a slave to *all*. Regarding lifestyle choices, decide what is important to you, your family, and your business, and then focus on executing based on those choices.

As always, I love to give examples or tell stories. I used to watch two reality shows that were both about two large families. While one of the two families had a fantastic kitchen in their house, I quickly noticed that they ate off of disposable Styrofoam plates for every meal. What I suspect is that they analyzed the cost of using disposable tableware for each meal versus the value of their time. For example, if it costs $10 for all of the paper products for a single meal versus taking 10 or more people 30 minutes to clean up, that expense is probably well worth it if they can afford it. So, in this case, the trade-off that they made was that their time was worth more than (1) the cost of the paper products, (2) the hassle of dealing with large amounts of trash, and (3) the possible impact on the environment—especially since they were using Styrofoam plates, which are one of the worst environmental offenders out there.

Another example concerns my wife and coupons. When we first got married, money was extremely tight. We were always looking for ways to stretch a dollar as far as possible. One of the things we did was to save and use coupons which was an idea that probably came from one or both of our sets of parents. Each week my wife would spend an hour looking through, cutting out, and organizing coupons. Each week I would have to deal with the huge Sunday newspaper that we never read. Periodically, I had to renew the membership for the newspaper and deal with the carrier when our coveted Sunday newspaper with the coupons did not arrive. All of this to save a few dollars on our grocery bill each month. When we truly looked at the time value of our money, it made no sense at all to coupon. We calculated we were stretching our grocery budget by no more than one percent. Therefore, we decided to bump-up our grocery budget by one percent and to cancel the newspaper subscription.

Reflecting back on this chapter, my goal from our family campouts was to connect more with nature. To that end, I tried to balance the trade-offs I was making. I chose to setup and use a three-tub KP setup so that we could be better stewards of the earth. I chose that my time before and during the campout was more important than my desire to minimize how much trash I ultimately put in the dumpster that was headed to the landfill. I think you get the point. What is important to others and their families is going to be different that for yours. What is key though is to know what you want, make choices that align with those desires, and then to not live in regret afterward.

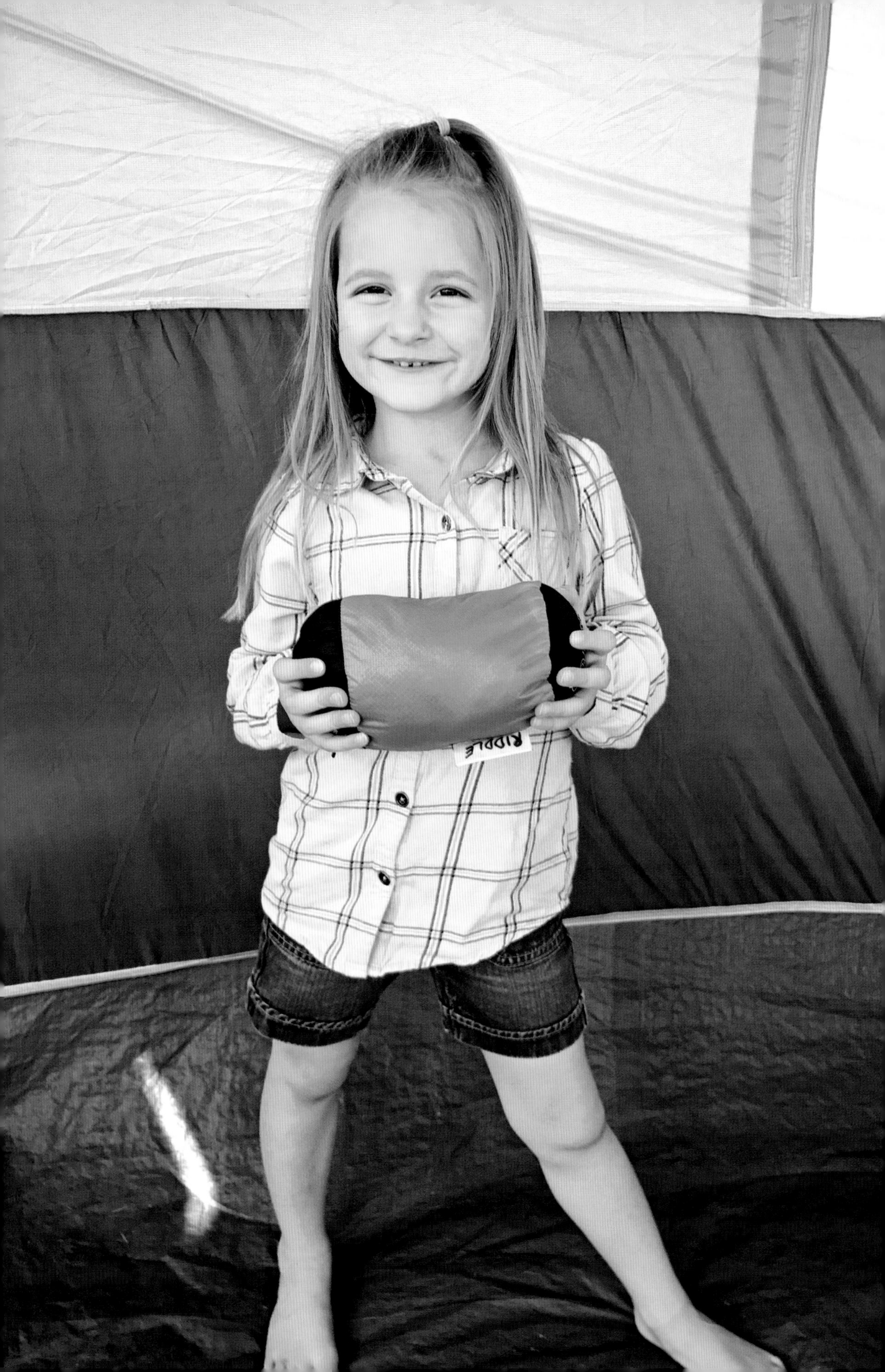

CHAPTER 7

SLEEPING

Having individual space is a must

Privacy is not usually something we think about much until you realize you do not have much of it. In the middle of the night on a campout is definitely *not* the time that you want to realize that you need your privacy in the form of your personal space. While your tent might be small and your funds might be tight, you should plan for everyone to have their own space in your family tent. Unless you and your spouse (or kids) sleep together on a double or queen air mattress every night at home, I would strongly suggest that you plan for everyone to have their personal space in the tent. This means their sleeping pad or air mattress, sleeping bag, pillow, and at least a few inches between everyone's sleeping pads.

If you have little ones, please plan for them to have their space as well. An exception to this will be if you have toddlers. In this case, you can have two toddlers share one sleeping pad. With each of them in their own tot-sized sleeping bag, arrange them so that their heads are at opposite ends of the sleeping pad and their lower legs and feet meet in the middle.

One time, when my youngest son was seven, and my second-youngest daughter was five, the three of us slept in my small backpacking tent that was only meant for two people. While I was okay on my XL sleeping pad, the two of them griped about not having their own space since I had the two of them sleep in one spot. But since it was a last-minute decision for my daughter to spend the night, it was a trade-off I could live with especially since I had only brought a small backpacking tent. My son, on the other hand, conveyed that he wished his sister had gone home with the rest of our crew. But since both fell sound asleep within 10 minutes of being in their sleeping bags, it all worked out fine.

If you and your spouse do want to sleep close, there are options where you can zip two exact sleeping bags together to make one bag, or you can

buy a fitted sheet, top sheet, and comforter set that fits a full or queen-sized air mattress relatively inexpensively. But unless you know beyond a shadow of a doubt that you and your sleeping partner can sleep this way, do not try to do so for the first time on a campout. Also, if you typically need to get up in the middle of the night to go to the bathroom, getting out of a shared sleeping bag or getting off a shared air mattress can be troublesome. Think through the ramifications carefully.

Please note that making sure everyone has their own personal space (and subsequently gets a good night's sleep) is one of those areas that, if you get it right the first and every subsequent time, nobody will ever know. Your crew will sleep through the night, wake up happy campers, and will be ready to move ahead with their day. But if you ask how your friends and their families slept, you will most likely hear less-than-stellar answers—primarily due to people not having their space. Go ahead and give yourself a pat on the back for being so wise—nobody else is going to since they will never know the careful thought you put into the subject of privacy and personal space while tenting together.

Sleeping pads are really nice to have

Thin they might be, but a luxury item they are not. Migrating to a self-inflating sleeping pad will probably be the single most important change that you can make that will improve your camping experience the most.

Over the years, I have tried many different options to get a better night's sleep on a campout. Whenever I have tried to cut corners on space, planning, or money, it has not yielded success in getting a better night's sleep. Trust me, you want to get a great night's sleep on a campout, and if possible, an even better sleep than you would at home. Once, I opted to bring a one-inch thick exercise mat instead of a sleeping pad. It was one of the worst night's sleep I ever had. Do not make this mistake yourself—exercise mats are not comfortable to sleep on.

Another time on a Cub Scout campout, it got down in the 30s during the night. The next morning over breakfast, I asked one of the moms how they had slept. She glared at me and said they had been extremely cold. I was confused because my family had slept great and had been warm and cozy all night. It turned out they had brought a shared air mattress—and nothing else. No sheets, no blankets, and no sleeping bags! The one and only time they had previously gone camping, it was in the summer when staying warm was not an issue. Unfortunately, they did not adjust their packing list to accommodate for the different season.

OK, so what is the big deal about a self-inflating pad? First, with its foam core, it will absorb, hold, and then radiate your heat back to you during the night. While you might think the secret is getting you off the ground since the coldest air sinks to ground level, that is not the primary factor involved here. Therefore, in the winter, cots and air mattresses are not the best choices. For cots, there is nothing under you holding the heat in. It is just like those bridges on the highway that have the signs that say "Bridge Might Freeze." With no dirt or ground under the bridge, the road surface can get very cold very quickly. The air mattress suffers from a similar problem. The air in the mattress quickly sucks the heat away from your body and transfers it to the air in the mattress, which, in turn, gets transferred to the ground or surrounding air—not back into your body.

A second advantage is that today's sleeping pads are self-inflating. Just open the valve(s) when you initially unroll them in your tent so that they can start to self-inflate. Then, right before you go to bed, blow five to 10 puffs in them, and you will be all set. Yes, it only does take that small amount of extra inflation. And third, they do not require any electricity, portable pump, extension cord, or fear that you might go into cardiac arrest trying to blow it up with your mouth. Finally, most sleeping pads are very small compared to a cot or air mattress when not in use. This fact can help if space is tight in your vehicle.

If you feel that you need to be higher off the ground due to your mobility needs (getting in and out of a cot), putting a sleeping pad on top of a cot is a great option. Just make sure the pad is not too big and does not hang off the edges of the cot.

The biggest difference I have noticed in the various sleeping pad thicknesses and whether they have been picked (foam removed in a geometric pattern to save on weight) is that your bottom will touch the ground when you sit on some of them. Regardless of the thickness, if you lie flat, you should not have any issue bottoming out. As far as sleeping goes, I have had good results on ones that range from two inches picked to 3.5 inches traditional.

The style of a sleeping bag versus its temperature rating

Mummy sleeping bags are rated to keep you from being cold down to -30 degrees. Is that what you need? I am often asked about how concerned should someone be about the rating of a sleeping bag versus its cost and what style would be most versatile. My experience with family camping in mild climates (30-degree lows to 100-degree highs) is that the style of the sleeping bag is much more important than anything else.

If a sleeping bag is not comfortable to you—no matter what the rating is—you will not have a good night's sleep. If you do not like the feel of silk sheets at home, you probably do not want a "slick" sleeping bag. If you prefer cotton

or flannel sheets and bedding at home, then you probably want a sleeping bag with a similar interior feel. Now, do not get me wrong—sleeping bags with specific ratings have a place and that place is on more extreme campouts (which is not the focus of this book on family camping). For instance, I have a sleep sack-style sleeping bag that I bring out during the hot summer months but have found that it is only appropriate when it is extremely hot (80 to 100 degrees at night). As soon as the night temperature cools off into the 70s, I am instantly too cold (or at least feel too cold). This is due to the slickness of the sack sucking my heat away via heat transfer.

My favorite sleeping bag is a very simple one that unzips from both sides and has ventilation zippers at the foot area and on the sides. It also has a zippered pocket for my phone and other items. For me, I usually like to go to bed feeling warm and thus, like to have the sleeping bag completely unzipped. This is problematic if it is a bag with only a side zipper. This forces me to flip my sleeping bag "top" onto the tentmate sleeping next to me or be crumbled into my valuable space. Also, in the middle of the night when I am still half asleep, it is sometimes hard to re-zip up a traditional one-zipper sleeping bag—especially if you have accidentally completely unzipped it and it is now off the track. That will not result in any fun—especially in the middle of the night. Therefore, I try to stay with the style that unzips on both the right and the left. With this style, I can then unzip and roll up the top beyond or at my feet when not needed. As usual, please look at my present sleeping bag recommendations on TheKeenCamper.com website.

A quick sleeping bag related story. Once, I woke up in the middle of the night to use the bathroom and noticed that while my 7-year-old son was sound asleep in his sleeping bag, his 3-year-old sister was completely gone. Fear set in, and I started to panic. I had strategically placed my sleeping bag between her and the tent's door to reduce the chance of her getting out of the tent without me knowing about it. Had someone come and taken her, or had she left the tent on her own? The bottom line was that she was GONE. I frantically searched her sleeping bag, and she was NOT there. More fear set in. I looked outside and still did not see her. Then, something told me to recheck her sleeping bag which I did. At the absolute very bottom of her sleeping bag, she was snuggled up in a ball. Then more fear set in—had she suffocated at the bottom of the bag? I placed my hand on her chest and felt it rise and fall with her breath. She was absolutely fine. She loved that sleeping bag! On the other hand, I have a 20-degree mummy bag that none of my kids will use. Why? Because it is slick and does not feel warm and cuddly like the one my daughter was hidden in.

A final concern is whether the sleeping bag is stuff-able. Kids (especially) when they are camping without you, absolutely hate sleeping bags that will only fit in their carrying bag/pouch if it is rolled in a very specific way. Therefore, either buy sleeping bags that are stuff-able and do not need to be rolled or buy an oversized stuff bag to use and stuff the sleeping bag in there the best that you can. If that still will not work, try to find the easiest-to-use straps you can find (such as ones with Velcro versus elaborate clasps) and teach your kids to roll up their sleeping bags the best they can. Having sleeping bags that everyone can pack up themselves will help make your life easier (since you will not have to do it all), will create togetherness, and will help your kids have a "can do it" sense of pride regarding this aspect of camping.

Here is a helpful hint related to sleeping bags. When we unpack upon arrival, we put the straps for each sleeping bag in the individual stuff bag that the sleeping bag came out of. After all the sleeping bags are out, we put all the bags (including the sleeping pad ones) in one single bag. This makes it much easier when we pack up because we know that all the bags are in one single bag and that all the straps are in their respective bags. After a few campouts, your family will get the hang of this and will appreciate this system you have orchestrated.

Should you bring your full-size pillow?

Packing a pillow is one of the most important steps to having a great campout experience. While people can quickly adjust to sleeping in a place other than their own bed, sleeping with a "bad pillow" can ruin your night's sleep, and then cause attitude issues that bleed over into the next day's mood.

If you are a new camper, I suggest bringing your regular pillow from home. This single item will make a huge difference in your sleep. Your pillow is so key that I recently read that people who travel a lot should get used to a travel pillow at home so that when they travel (and take it with them), they will already be used to it.

After you have camped for a while, you can migrate to a camping pillow. You will want to do this for a couple of reasons. First, so you do not need to bring your full-size (or queen/king) pillow on the campout and risk it gets soiled or ruined. Second, and most importantly, due to the small footprint a camping pillow provides, it is a much better solution since your vehicle is already going to be jammed pack. My preferred camping pillows are those made from foam cubes. These foam cubes are left over from the manufacturing process for self-inflating sleep pads when the excess foam is trimmed from the edges of those pads.

Please note that foam camping pillows are at their fullest and maximum size right after they have been machine washed and dried. Once you roll it up, it never quite returns to that size until it is washed and machine dried again. Therefore, I try my best to keep my pillow unrolled on the way to the campout. When packing up on Sunday, I do roll it up though. This works out fine since we typically wash it when we get home since our hair was usually dirty when we slept on it at night.

If you do take your camping pillow rolled-up to the campout, please make sure that as soon as you get your tent set up and your gear put in the tent, that you unroll your pillow. This will give it at least a few hours to partially fluff up. It is absolutely the pits to get in bed, and then realize that you forgot to do this.

Also, please avoid blow-up pillows. The word pillow should never be associated with the word blow-up. These two concepts just do not work well together. If you have not tried one, blow-up pillows tend to be very "hard." With that said, I have successfully used ones that are a combination of self-inflating foam with an inflatable membrane though. While these too are still not my preference, they are an excellent way to save even more space since they can close into the size of your fist.

Change your clothes before going to sleep

Maybe it's just a guy thing, but I tend to sleep in my clothes when I camp. First, if I need to get up in the middle of the night to take someone to the restroom or to chase off a bear, I am all set and ready to go. Second, when I get up in the morning, I am already dressed for the day. In the colder weather, I do change every bit of clothing, including my underwear, before I go to bed though. I do this to avoid feeling colder than necessary during the night. Even on the coldest day, I know that my body still sweat/perspired. At night, the moisture in that sweat will tend to get very cold, and being pressed up to my body in cotton clothes, it can cause me to be unnecessarily cold. This, in turn, can cause a person to get sick. Everything I put on will be part of my outfit for the next morning/day. I do tend to sleep in shorts the entire year, so in the winter, I will change my shorts for pants in the morning. But other than that, I am completely ready to go in the morning. If my clothes are soiled or dirty, I do not sleep in them. But I will change into similar clean versions before I go to sleep. My wife and my kids bring pajamas and sleep in them. For my older son who is used to tenting with other boys his age, he sleeps in his clothes as well. And, yes, your shirt is going to be more wrinkled in the morning, but that is just what it is.

Inexpensive fleece blankets improve your sleeping bag's temperature rating

Air pockets have helped me and my family stay warm on many cold camping nights. While we do live in Texas, and it very rarely gets down into the 20s (and especially not when we are camping), we have been able to effectively use our inexpensive multi-season sleeping bags to stay warm.

While somewhat cumbersome and bulky, we use 4x6-foot inexpensive fleece/acrylic blankets to help us stay warm. When my little ones are ready for bed, I have them stand up and wrap them up (loosely) like a burrito. Then, I unzip their sleeping bag and have them lay down in it, and then zip it back up for them. I do have them extend their arms like a cross and wrap the blanket under their arms  and not over them. For me, I just lay the blanket over my legs and torso after I get in my sleeping bag and then zip it back up.

So, what is going on with all of this? The secret is the creation of air pockets. Let's think back to your house and the insulation that is used there. Consider the pink wispy or blown insulation that is used. Household insulation has an R-value rating which conveys how good of an insulator it is. One factor that improves the R-value is how tall or high the insulation is. Once stepped on and compressed, that R-value changes and the ability to insulate effectively goes down significantly. The reason is that the insulation works off the concept of trapped air pockets.

Now, let's think about your sleeping bag. There is one huge air pocket around your body inside the bag that is not very effective at holding in heat. But as that fleece blanket bunches itself up, a multitude of air pockets are created. Maybe a couple of inches by your right-hand side, a bunched area by your arm, etc. Inside these bunches is trapped air. And these trapped air cells can create a lot of additional insulation. In my experience, an inexpensive sleeping bag with an inexpensive fleece blanket can easily keep you warm even when the temperature is down in the lower 30s.

The benefits of using a sleeping bag liner

Washable sleeping bag liners are fantastic. The only real downside to them is how expensive some are. A sleeping bag liner is essentially a very, very long pillowcase that someone can fit their entire body into. Some have been professionally engineered/designed and use high-tech specialized fabrics, while others are standard polyester or cotton. They all have several great purposes, though.

First, in warmer weather, they can be used stand-alone as a super-lightweight sleeping bag. While you can certainly buy sleeping bag liners from camping

and outdoor retailers, you can also buy a product that has a little more versatility. It is called "The Original Dreamie" and was originally sold on late-night *As Seen on TV* ads. It is essentially a sleeping bag liner. They are intended for you to spend the night at someone's house when you need to sleep on their couch or floor and do not want to have contact with a fabric surface (that might not be clean). When I took a group of older boys to the Bahamas for a week to work on a sailboat, many of them slept on the deck of the ship and used only a sleeping bag liner on top of a sleeping pad.

The second benefit is that if your kids go to bed on the campout somewhat dirty without having taken a shower, the liner is what they will come in contact—not the sleeping bag. Therefore, when you get home, all that you will need to do is to wash the liner and not the entire sleeping bag. The challenge is convincing a child that is probably exhausted (and not bothered at all about going to bed horribly dirty) that they need to slide into the sleeping bag liner inside their sleeping bag.

Also, the liners are good in place of using fleece blankets during the winter to provide additional insulation. The advantage over the blanket is that most liners compress down to a size just a little larger than an adult male's fist. The bad news is some are very narrow and thus, can feel very confining—especially if you want to turn on your side while sleeping. Also, they can be a little bit difficult to get back into in the middle of the night. In fact, I have agonized in the middle of the night if I genuinely needed to go to the bathroom bad enough to make the hassle of getting back into my sleeping bag liner worth it.

The liners that are not stretchable and more "slick" feeling are usually very cheap. The ones that have more cotton (think how a super soft t-shirt feels) and are stretchable can get very pricey; sometimes, they cost as much as a sleeping bag. Also, many of the pricey ones come with some form of built-in chemical insect repellent and anti-odor/bacterial feature. Because there are chemicals involved, please determine if these are appropriate for your family and children. And finally, be mindful that over time and with multiple washes, these chemicals might become less effective.

Cover your head during the winter when you sleep

Unfamiliar with how to stay warm when camping in cold weather, my kids and I suffered unnecessarily during our first year or so of family camping.

Going off what I had learned while in Boy Scouts as a youth (which turned out to not be very aligned with today's generally accepted camping knowledge), I relied solely on my sleeping bag and air mattress/cot/exercise mat to stay warm. It turned out this was not the correct approach.

Eventually, I found out that you lose most of your heat at night (and maybe during the day as well) through your head. Your head acts like a giant lightbulb or radiator, radiating a great deal of your heat away from your body at night. On winter hikes as a youth, I had always focused on keeping my torso covered so that the blood being pumped by my heart throughout my body was warm. As an adult, I subsequently and incorrectly took that approach while sleeping—that if I kept my torso covered I would be sufficiently warm on a cold night. Through the advice and counsel of others, I came to understand my big mistake was not keeping my head covered at night.

Now, my entire family sleeps with some form of ski cap when we camp in the winter. While inexpensive knit/crotchet-style ones are sufficient, I have a high-tech one that works great. The main downside to wearing ski caps to bed is that I wake up in the morning feeling like my hair and face are very dirty. Since my skin can get oily during the night, having my hair pressed against my scalp all night causes the oil to transfer to my hair as well. Sorry if this is too much information, but I just want you to know the shortcomings of wearing caps to bed. Also, during the night, I sometimes feel very confined since I am not used to sleeping with a cap except on campouts. If you can find a ski cap that has flaps that scoop down over your ears, these are even better. Wearing ski caps to bed on cold nights has helped us stay warm more than anything else except for the self-inflating sleeping pads which are vitally important as well.

Fans can help when it is hot and/or humid

Whatever you need to do to have a good night's sleep on your campout is the path I would recommend. Since sleep is so important, you need to get a solid night's sleep. If possible, it would be great if you could achieve a level

that is better than at home. That way, the entire family campout experience for your family will be perceived as being that much better. When you can have a better night's sleep while getting back to nature, it can be very inspiring. On the other hand, having a bad night's sleep will keep you from coming back and will cause the next day to probably not be the best. Getting the right amount of sleep is critical.

So, while battery-powered fans are not very outdoorsy, please use them if you need to. At home, my wife and I are used to having a ceiling fan on in our bedroom. My two sons are used to having a fan that sits on their floor. So, even if it is not hot, the fact of merely having air blow across you might be what you require to fall and stay asleep. If you are used to a fan at home, you are going to need something to circulate air in your tent.

While you should look at my present recommendations for specific manufacturers and models on the TheKeenCamper.com website, I recommend finding a fan that:

- ☀ Has 10-inch fan blades
- ☀ Can be operated with an AC adapter
- ☀ Comes with a 12-volt car adapter
- ☀ Can be operated with batteries
- ☀ Has a base that allows it to stand on its own
- ☀ Has an attached hook so that it can be hung from above

If you are camping in the summer, having a fan to cool things down so that you can fall asleep is imperative. Having air blowing across your body (especially if you perspire) can lower the effective temperature you are experiencing by several degrees.

My sons and I have used battery-operated fans at Webelos Resident Camp for four years now. If you go with the battery option, it can get a little pricey. Make sure to get a fan that has both AC and 12-volt adapters included. If your fan does not come with these adapters and you decide to purchase them separately, it could be as high as 30 percent of the original cost of the fan. Most take eight D-cell batteries each. So, if you bring a set of eight D-cell batteries, plus an entire set of eight spares, you will get close to spending as much on batteries as you did on the original fan.

Also, I have found that you need one fan per person. Trying to position a small fan like this so that it can blow a sufficient amount of air across multiple people just does not work. Do not even try it. Nobody will be much better off, and you still would have incurred the expense. The only exception is with smaller kids. They will be worn out by the end of the day and are probably going to fall asleep regardless. Therefore, I am mainly talking about you, your spouse, and middle/high school-aged kids.

Due to the high cost of batteries, I would suggest investing in a car charger to power your AC adapter (or the 12-volt car adapter). Also, bring something to set the fans on to get them up off the ground (so that you can better direct their air flow). I have seen people set them on upside-down 5-gallon buckets as well as foot lockers. Even if your fan comes with a built-in hook, you should bring a small rope or zip ties to more securely connect it to your tent. Also, please be mindful of the weight of the fan and look for signs that this weight is not damaging your tent. If your fan does not have an included hook, you can use zip ties to loop through the slit openings to create something to hang the fan by as well.

Plan for needing to go to the bathroom during the middle of the night

You need to get past any embarrassment regarding this subject. Going to the bathroom is a normal thing. If you need to use the bathroom during the middle of the night at home, then you are most likely going to need to do the same on a campout.

And, yes, you probably wish you could do it in private, but, come on, this is *your* family. Whether it is sitting on a camping toilet in the middle of your tent in the dark, urinating into a jar if you are a guy, or needing to leave the tent to use a real bathroom, it should not be a big deal. Regarding taking care of your business in the tent, first, nobody is going to be up to see you—they should all be asleep. And, second it is going to be too dark for anyone to see you anyway should they be awake.

Speaking of darkness and lighting, at home you most likely do not need to turn on a light to find your way to the bathroom since it is something you have learned to do over time without light. On a campout though, you are most likely going to need a flashlight to find your way out of the tent or to find your way to the camping toilet in the tent. I would suggest a light source that is bright enough (or in a different color such as red) that you can see what you are doing but not so bright that it wakes up your tentmates.

Trying just to hold my pee (when I did not have a place inside the tent to go) has never worked out for me. It is painful, not healthy, and will keep you from falling back asleep. The options are pretty simple. Either have something in your tent you can pee into or plan to leave the tent in the middle of the night. If you are going to do the latter, slip on a pair of flip-flops, walk away from the tent a few feet, and then go. While I know there will probably be some haters on this subject, my opinion is that you need to do what you need to do.

Also, from what I have seen, the kids tend to sleep throughout the night, and it is only the parents that need to go the bathroom overnight. With that said, you should probably be prepared to take your kids to the actual campground bathroom first thing in the morning since kids usually need to go when they first wake up.

Personal lighting during the night

Unnecessarily bright lights will not only wake you out of a REM sleep but can also wake up others in your tent. Since the focus of this book is family camping, it is very likely that some members of your family might go to sleep earlier than others. At a minimum, you and your spouse might not be finished with your bedtime rituals by the time everyone is ready to fall asleep. What usually happens with us is that as soon as the kids hit their sleeping bags, they are out cold. At that point, my wife and I still need to brush our teeth, get our sleeping clothes on, and do various other end-of-the-night  tasks. So, we try to keep the tent more dimly lit. Realistically, since the kids did completely fall asleep with the lights full on, we probably do not need to dim the lights at all—but it just feels like we should. In this situation, there are two items that I suggest. The first is a headlamp. The headlamp will let you keep light where you need it. But you will need to be cautious of where your head is pointing, though—especially if it is toward one of your sleeping family members. If you are not careful, you could end up shining a 100+ lumen light straight at their face.

The second item I suggest is an inflatable lantern. Most are about five inches in diameter and five inches tall. They use LEDs and usually have translucent/frosted plastic sides that do a great job of illuminating an area but not flooding it with light. They usually can dim the light across a relatively wide spectrum, as well. These lanterns are great in the middle of the night if you need to have a light but do not want to wake up anyone else (or even yourself more fully). If you can find one where the light is under 0.3W, that would be even better.

Use earplugs, beauty masks & medication to take the edge off

While starlit windy nights can elicit a very romantic image of the outdoors, quite often, these things can keep you from getting a good night's sleep. Although I am a pretty sound sleeper, at home, all that I hear is the water from my saltwater fish tank and the circulating air from my ceiling fan. In the wilderness, I have found these different sounds often tend to bother me and keep me from falling (and staying) asleep. Therefore, I have gotten used to wearing foam earplugs. These are also great in case someone you are camping with snores. Even while wearing earplugs, I have camped with a few people who snored so loudly that I could still hear them—even though their tent was 30 feet away!

In fact, the way that I got turned on to foam earplugs was via a snorer. We were camping with my older son's Cub Scout pack and were getting ready to go to bed. One of the other dads said he was going to bed and that there were some packs of foam earplugs in a chair in front of his tent. I thought how odd that he was telling me this and what a weird way to say good night. About 30 minutes later, I found out why. As I was working to fall asleep, I heard an awful sound—it was him snoring! I proceeded to unzip my tent and walk barefoot, tippy-toe-style, across the hard and rocky ground to the chair in front of his tent. I grabbed a pair of earplugs and headed back to my tent to figure out how to put them in my ears. Oh, my goodness—did they ever help!

The secret with the foam earplugs is to not insert them directly into your ear canal. Instead, you need to twist them so that they become slightly compressed. *Then*, you insert them into your ears. As they expand, they completely eliminate almost all sounds. Be warned—it will take you a while to get used to how very, very quiet it will be when wearing them. Sometimes, it is so quiet that you will be able to hear your heartbeat. So, please try to practice with these at home—both, how to insert them and to get used to how quiet it will be. Also, you will need to remind your kids and spouse that they will need to talk directly into your ear (within just an inch) if they want you to hear them.

Please note the following about wearing foam earplugs. When I use them, I always place myself between the tent door and my kids. I do this in case they try to leave during the middle of the night, or someone else attempts to enter the tent. With how well they work, it is possible that you might not hear someone enter or leave your tent in the middle of the night. Another option is to attach bear "bells" on the tent zipper pulls.

Finally, I also do two other things to help improve my night's sleep and reduce how the different sounds impact me. First, I take two allergy pills to help knock me out. I do this since the side effect of most allergy medicine is drowsiness. Please note that you should seek the advice of your doctor before trying this approach. And, depending on how your body handles allergy medicine, you might negatively impact your next day if you are still feely drowsy. Second, I bring a beauty mask should there be any stray lights (from campground street lamps) or if the moon is out and very full. The bottom line is that it is going to take a few campouts to get all of this figured out and what works best for you. Each of your family members (at least the older ones) will probably require a different regime of what helps them to get a better night's sleep. They key is to find out what that regime is and then to use it faithfully.

Take advantage of the dark by going to bed early

Wasteful is often the word that I think of when I think about going to bed early. Unfortunately, I have struggled for years with the bad habit of not going to bed at home until the wee hours of the morning. While my thought process is that I have too much to do and can stay up and get a little more done, that is seldom the case. I usually end up not being near as productive as I had hoped. Since all my *To Do's* are back at home, I have fortunately had better success going to bed when I should on campouts.

Unless you arrived late on the first day of your campout and are still setting up camp, after dinner is over (and cleaned up), you should, theoretically, be able to hit the sack—assuming that it is already dark since going to bed on a campout while it is still light is pretty hard to do. The only reason that I would suggest staying up late on a campout is to fellowship with others. Sitting around a campfire having a hot drink (coffee, tea, or hot chocolate) with my friends or wife has provided some of my fondest memories.

So, with all of this said, clean up dinner, let your kids play some fun nighttime games (capture the flag, cards, etc.), sit around fellowshipping with your friends, and then go to bed earlier than usual. If you do, you will most likely wake up feeling much more refreshed and able (and willing) to start your day when the sun comes up.

Is it OK to have water and snacks in your tent?

This is an extremely tough one for me. As mentioned elsewhere in this chapter, getting a great night's sleep is super important—especially for the person who is the primary parent and will lead most of the next day's activities for everyone else. So, I try to get my sleep experience as close to what it's like at home. Unfortunately, for me, this means having a bottle of water on my nightstand and the ability to walk to the kitchen to a get a middle-of-the-night snack if I wake up hungry.

Also, if your little ones are used to having a small snack before bed, this could be problematic if they are already in the tent for the evening. So, here is what I typically do. First, I do bring a water bottle into the tent but do try to bring one in a container that does not condensate or is at room temperature. Even with this precaution, I have seen ants find their way into tents to find water from the condensation. Honestly, I do not know how they are getting in—somehow, they squeeze through the seams or mesh. Also, I know that some snakes such as copperheads will hunt incessantly for water in the hotter, dry summer months. I have not heard of snakes getting into closed tents, though.

Regarding food, I must admit that I occasionally will bring a factory-sealed bag of trail mix, raisins, or nuts in the tent and will eat it in one mouthful, and then will throw the wrapper outside the tent. While I am trying to work on not having to snack in the middle of the night at home, until then, I will probably still feel the need to have a snack during the night on campouts. When I get this under control at home, I will then stop doing this on campouts. Bringing any food (including sealed prepackaged food) into the tent is just a bad idea. Is it worth having to buy a new tent or backpack after a wild animal has clawed their way in? The answer should be "no." In fact, I have heard of stories where animals chewed through a tent wall, and then through the side of a backpack to get to an apple or other similar food (that was in a backpack). Destroying a tent and a backpack (that might have cost several hundred dollars), plus possibly having a disease-laden wild animal in your tent is *not* worth it. If you do get hungry during the night, put on your shoes and headlamp, leave your tent to find something to eat, and have your snack outside the tent. As a side note, I have found that drinking water can fill you up if you do get hungry in the middle of the night. Therefore, that might be a much alternative to bringing food into your tent.

Bunk cots can help large families

If you have a large family, then bunk cots are a great way to go. Until a few years ago, bunk cots were not commercially available and were primarily only used by the military in situations where they needed to quickly mobilize troops. While not trying to specifically call out one brand over another, I honestly only know of one bunk cot manufacturer at this time. It is Disc-O-Cot (or Camp-O-Cot).

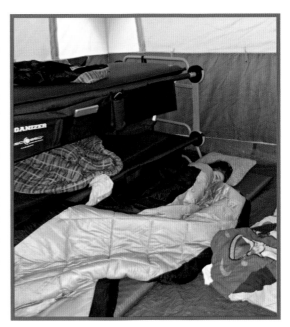

The advantage of a bunk cot is that you can fit two people into the footprint of one person in a tent and still have storage space under the bottom cot. My wife and I have a large family, which includes the two of us and five kids. For this reason, we use a large 10x14-foot tent that is meant for nine campers. Since that number *nine* is meant to mean nine people sleeping right next to each other in sleeping bags without sleeping pads, that is not going to result in nine (and not even seven) happy campers.

When all seven of us camp together without our bunk cots, we must sleep in multiple different directions, and still, there is absolutely no room to walk/ move around or to put our personal gear bags. And no matter how hard we try not to, someone eventually gets stepped on. Therefore, we now bring our bunk cots whenever we bring our big family tent.

The Disc-O-Cot brand of bunk cots also comes with a neat add-on side panel. This panel connects via Velcro and provides places for your water bottle, electronics, wallet, book, etc.

The downsides to the bunk cots are the cost, weight (a set of two cots weighs 64 lbs), and the fact that they require a good amount of room inside your tent when assembling and dissembling them. After a round of training, though, my 15-year-old son now takes care of putting them together and taking them down. In fact, we just recently purchased a second set of bunk cots. We place each set on opposite sides of the tent, which allows us to have three people comfortably sleeping in the middle.

While you could use them without a pad, I like to use a self-inflating pad on top of my bunk for two reasons. First, it is a more comfortable night's sleep. Second, it provides more adequate insulation during cold months (when the coldest air in the tents is directly under the cots). Once again, think of how bridges ice quicker than the roads in the winter since there is only air underneath them.

Also, since they are fairly uncommon due to the cost and the fact that most people do not have large families, they provide a real conversation piece when people realize you have them. And like always, this allows you to have wonderful conversations with others about your shared love of camping.

What lessons in leading your family can you take away from this aspect of camping?

"Rest"

As you hopefully surmised, I am a big proponent of getting enough rest via a good night's sleep. Unfortunately, I am a much-better advocate than I am a role model for doing so. What is interesting is that I do a much, much better job on campouts than I do at home with getting the right amount of sleep. While I am not an expert by any means regarding all the benefits of getting a solid night's sleep and how to achieve a sleep nirvana, I do know enough basics to understand how important it is.

From a campout perspective, I want you and your family to have the absolute best time you can. With all the planning, work, and preparation you are going to put into it, I want you to maximize the experience. Being tired on Saturday morning after your first night at camp, with your kids ready to go full steam ahead, is not desirable. But, getting the best night's sleep on a campout does not happen by accident or by magic. Instead, it comes from deliberate steps you take ahead of time.

The same is true in your everyday life. And in everyday life, the impact is even larger. First, if you have a pattern of not getting enough sleep, the incremental negative impact will eventually impact your life in real ways. Second (and probably more importantly), you are setting a bad lifestyle example for your family. What your kids (and your spouse) learn from your example has a high chance of carrying over into their everyday life as adults.

At a high level, here is what I know about rest via sleep:

- ☀ Everyone needs a different amount, and that amount varies by age.
- ☀ In general, people need between seven to eight hours per night.
- ☀ Sleep that is split across multiple time slots (a few hours here and a few hours there) is not the same as a continuous night's sleep.
- ☀ You need some amount of deep REM sleep.
- ☀ Not getting enough sleep is tied to craving unhealthy foods the following day.

- ☀ Not getting enough sleep can lead to weight control issues.

- ☀ Not getting enough sleep leaves you unable to operate at your best—which can lead to being depressed, grumpy, not having clarity, and not being able to enjoy everything before you.

I would argue that not getting enough sleep is truly an addiction. After a while of starving yourself from sleep, your body and mind start to believe that is the norm. But unlike other addictions like alcohol and drugs, the impact is less in your face. Nevertheless, the damage is still occurring.

Among my family's pets, we have two birds. One is a cockatiel, and the other is a yellow-shouldered Amazon parrot. Our vet continues to remind us that they both need at least 10 hours of sleep. To do that, we would need to get them to bed by 8 p.m.—which never happens. And getting them to bed means placing their cages in a quiet, dark place with the cages covered with a blanket or cloth. Unfortunately, we struggle with this because we enjoy interacting with them, and the evening is one of the main times we can do so. Whenever we tell the vet that they are wide awake and appear to want to interact with us late at night, she reminds us that *we* are the responsible adults (and the humans) and need to make better choices for them. I think you can see how this situation can be extended to your kids as well. Of course, your kids seem excited about staying up late, but what do they know? They are just kids and still need your guidance.

My recommendation is to educate yourself on the benefits of getting the right amount of sleep and then do what you can do to achieve it. The sky is the limit. There are so many thoughts about factors like temperatures, scents, ceiling fans, background music, and white noise to choose from. In parallel to this, make a conscious decision to commit to getting enough sleep. With that said, I suggest trying the following process:

- ☀ Decide how much sleep you need.

- ☀ Decide what time you need to get up to have a successful day.

- ☀ Back up the hours you need from your rise time, and that is your new bedtime. From there back up enough time to do your hygiene, lock the house, and get things ready for the next day.

Now, for the hard part. You are *not* going to be able to get near as much done as you have been. But by holding sleep as an absolute, you will figure out, over time, what to reprioritize and what to cut out. And while it might feel like you are losing out, in the long run (if you stick to this), the positive benefits will be significant.

And think about the things your kids will learn from you as they see you making better lifestyle choices. So, start making *rest* a higher priority in your life today.

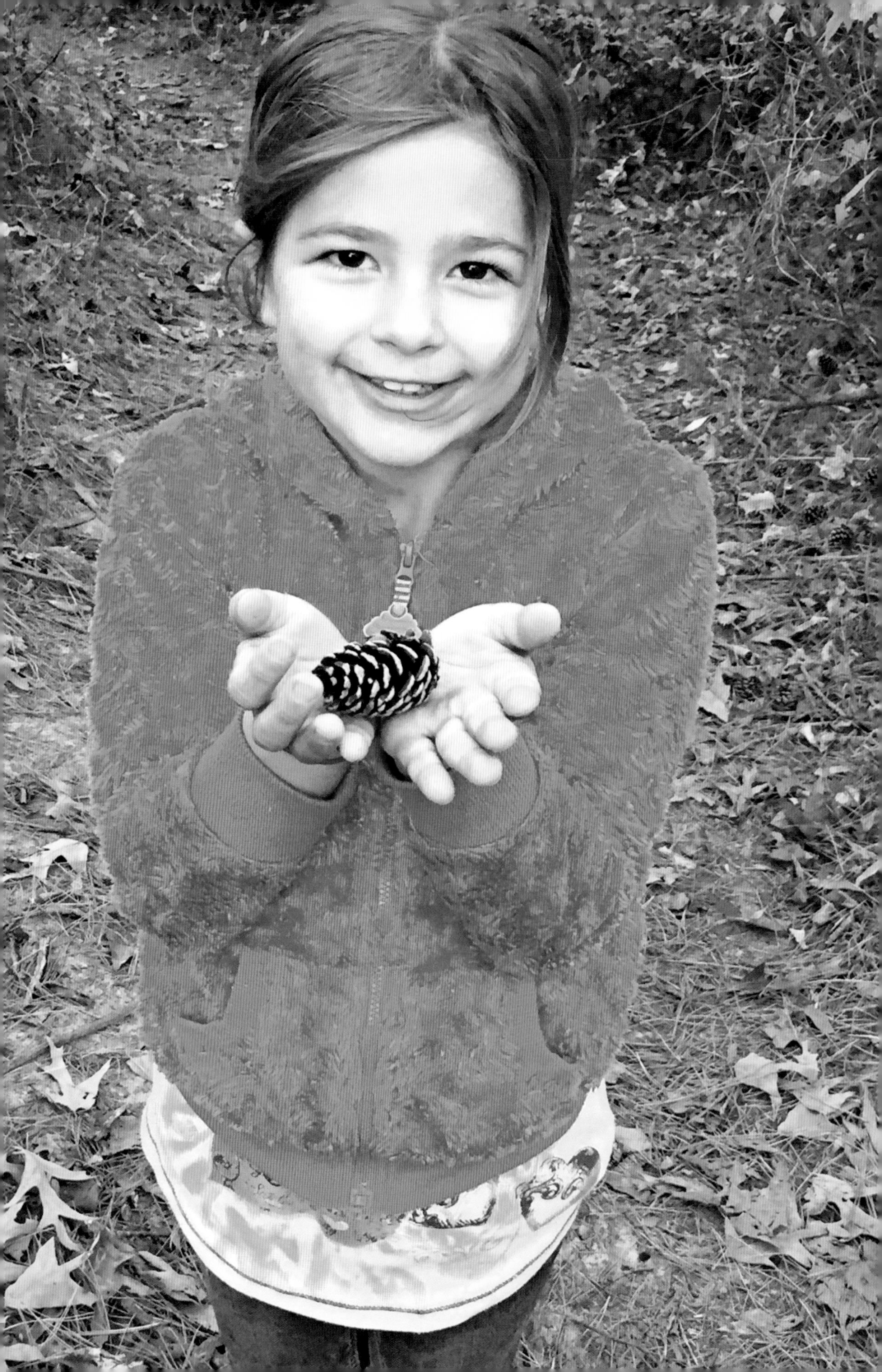

CHAPTER 8

DO OUTDOOR STUFF

Make it different than being at home

The advice that I am about to offer here is relevant to almost anything that you do. If you go somewhere or do anything special and end up doing the exact same things that you normally do at home, then what is the point?

Years ago, on a Cub Scout campout, there was a man who was camping with us with his two sons. For the entire weekend, he sat in a chair and read a book and did e-mail via his phone. No kidding—he did not interact with any of us (or even his sons) all weekend long. What was the point of coming if he did not participate in any of the activities and missed out experiencing them with his two sons?

Do not get me wrong—I understand that there will occasionally be times when you will need to do work associated with your job. It is not uncommon in today's highly-connected and fast-paced world for someone to only be able to attend if they can periodically check-in with their work. For example, we had a father who took his family on a family campout with us, and he was in the final days of running a Kickstarter campaign for a board game his company was trying to get funded and released. Even with this going on, he still came. He set up his laptop outside on a picnic table and participated in many activities with his kids and wife. He is the example of the way it should be done. The people I am challenging to do differently are the ones who come on a campout and continue to do the same normal things and have (or let) their children do the same activities as back at home. The good news is that it does not have to be this way. What follows are my ideas on how you can break out of this bad habit.

Here are some things to try:

- ☀ Cook meals over an open fire
- ☀ Stay up way too late by a campfire
- ☀ Drink water from a natural spring
- ☀ Swim in a lake
- ☀ Take a hike every morning
- ☀ Read a book in a hammock

If all that you have done is temporarily relocate your home to the campground for the weekend and do the same things—like watching college football on your iPad or updating Facebook, once again, what is the point?

Here are some more ideas:

- ☀ If you normally rise early, try sleeping in late.
- ☀ If you normally do not have dessert at home, not only have dessert but have seconds.
- ☀ If you normally drink sodas, then drink water.

Do things that are different from what you do back at home. If your life at home is stressed and overscheduled, then do activities that are more in-line with chilling, relaxing, and enjoying the outdoors.

While in the outdoors do outdoor activities

Like my above suggestion about doing different things on campouts than you would at home, I also strongly suggest that you do as many outdoor things as possible. For some of you, this will be very natural and could already be part of your norm. For others, you are going to need to get a little out of your comfort zone. This chapter will highlight some easy and cost-effective things you can do in the outdoors. Unless the weather is lousy, you should not be spending any time in your tent during the day. That is unless you have chosen to take a nap and do not have a hammock or another method to take a nap in the fresh open air.

Sitting, lying, and resting are acceptable—just do them outside, if possible. As you make choices, think about how your kids would answer, or better yet, illustrate the answer to the following question when they return to school on Monday: "What did your parents do this weekend?" Would they draw a picture of you outside doing something best suited for the outdoors or sitting in a camping chair reading e-mail on your smartphone?

For my older son's first Boy Scout Summer Camp, we went to a camp near Colorado Springs. While I had been encouraged to enroll him in a "first-year" Scout program, we decided not to. The reason being is that those first-year boys were going to be sitting on benches in front of a teepee for an entire week learning about basic Scout skills. I told my wife that when our son returns home from camp, I wanted him to be able to tell us how Colorado was. So, we suggested he take horseback riding and canoeing classes. Both classes would get him outside and enjoying the outdoors.

At the same summer camp, we had some Scouts that wanted to spend their free time reading books in their tents. While I am a huge fan of reading, I just would not like to see it happen to the detriment of other fun campout activities. While these boys are to be commended for knowing what they enjoyed doing and were taking control of their circumstances, it would have been better if they had found a shaded spot under a tree or sat in a camping chair than being inside their tent with the tent flaps closed. Also, it would have been better to have not made this their primary activity. One idea would have been to relegate their reading to the early morning or the late evening.

On yet another occasion, we had one of the older boys in our Boy Scout troop spend the entire weekend playing cards in a heated recreation hall we rented for a winter campout. The intent was to use this building only for sleeping at night and for the boys to spend their days outside just like on a regular campout. The issue was not him playing cards but that it was the *only* thing he wanted to do—and he proceeded to do it all day long inside.

Once again, think about the picture your kids would draw of your camping weekend. Will you be depicted holding your smartphone or doing an activity best suited for home?

Ideas for observing nature

Unfortunately, I have a challenging time following the next bit of advice. It is to make sure to observe nature. The way that I am wired, I sometimes struggle with being or living in the moment, and thus, spend a good deal of my thoughts thinking about what is next. While this is a great quality for staying on top of things, unfortunately, you do miss out on a lot of what makes life special which tends to happen in the moment.

When you are outside camping, make sure that you are mentally noting all the wonderful natural things such as trees, leaves, and even the way a trail

meanders through the woods. How the stars shine so much brighter at night in the countryside against a background that is truly black. How the birds chirp in the morning and the frogs croak at night against the orchestra of crickets.

There is so much beauty out there in nature, and it all works together and doesn't need us at all. So much of our city life depends on us. Kids need us to fix dinner, cars need us to put gas in them—it seems like everyone needs "us." But nature does not. It already has everything it needs and does *not* need us—in fact, it probably even prefers us not to be around.

As you notice these wonderful "natural" things, point them out to your kids, saying things like, "Look at how tall that tree is" or "That is a neat-looking bird, isn't it?" Here are the key basics to get started:

- ☀ Just start noticing things yourself.
- ☀ For the truly unique things, point them out to your family.
- ☀ Do not worry about not knowing the specifics. You can enjoy looking at a beautiful tree even if you do not know what type it is.
- ☀ Take lots of pictures.

Over time, you should try to get more informed about the outdoors and nature though. Learning how to identify animals, scat, plants, and constellations will all help you to become more literate and to better appreciate and enjoy the outdoors.

Collecting butterflies and other insects

I have never been a big "bug" person, but a Scout I know and his father (to a lesser degree) are totally obsessed with bugs. When we go on campouts together, this young man brings a collapsible butterfly habitat and containers to transport bugs back home. He not only enjoys spotting and identifying them, but he also loves taking them home to add them to his collection. At home, he has several huge pieces of Styrofoam that he has pinned dead bugs on. Also, on campouts, he brings some cotton balls that have been dipped in a chemical that painlessly kills these bugs. He puts an insect in a container, puts one of these chemical-soaked cotton balls in, and waits for it to stop moving (which is an indication that it is now dead).

If you are not into collecting specimens of bugs, you can do it like the Pokémon Snap video game that was designed years ago for the Nintendo 64 platform. In this game, you "capture" animals with your camera by taking pictures of them. Also, it is highly likely that there are applications for your smartphone that let you photograph and catalog your "virtual" insect collection.

To make it a more interesting experience, I would learn about the most common insects in your local area for two primary reasons. First, so that you can highlight them to your kids as you see them. Second, it is probably good to know which ones are dangerous and which are just annoying. There all sorts of books, apps, brochures, flash cards, and even playing cards that can  be used to help you learn how to identify various insects. While you might not ever become enamored by bugs to the extent that you want to take them home with you, you will at least be more informed about them.

Finally, if bugs are just too gross for you to deal with, focus on butterflies. For most people, butterflies elicit good thoughts and feelings while traditional insects and bugs do not.

You want me to become a bird watcher too?

Just like with the insects, start off slow. In the beginning, just focus on stopping and noticing them. Compared to at home in an urban or suburban environment, you will see so many more varieties of birds on campouts. At first, it will be "hey, look at that pretty red bird." Eventually, you will hopefully move on to "look at that male northern Red-headed woodpecker." Unlike insects, you probably should not (and especially since it is probably illegal too) collect physical examples of birds. But you can note them in a notebook you have, take pictures, or even sketch them.

If you are like me, you probably did not realize there were so many varieties of birds right here in your "backyard." In the cities, there sometimes are only the varieties that are heartier and have gotten used to having virtually no natural habitat. But in the woods on a campout, there tends to be a much-greater variety.

Besides learning to identify birds by their looks, you can also learn to identify them by their sounds, their nests, or even the artifacts they leave behind (like holes in a tree from a woodpecker).

If you camp with families (possibly even your own) that hunt and fish, they tend to bring a lot to the hobby of bird watching. For example, we were camping with another family, and their 14-year-old son pointed out a bird that was on the ground about 20 feet away from me that was squawking. He said it was trying to make me think that it was injured by its call. He also said that its wing was not injured, but that it was holding it in a manner to make me believe it was broken. He said that this variety of bird laid its eggs on the ground, and because of that, was trying to get me to move toward it and away from her eggs by pretending to be injured. It was incredibly neat. And to think this came from a well-informed youth who had learned this from his father who was an avid outdoorsman.

You will also get a chance to "observe" less desirable birds too. On a campout at Purtis Creek State Park here in Texas, we had trouble with a whip-poor-will that was making noise all night. When we would get out of our tents and toss rocks toward it and shout into the night, it would eventually move on. But then later in the night, it would come back. What we did not realize was that it was only moving on to the campsite right next to ours. And our next-door camping neighbors were, in turn, shooing it back to us after we had, inadvertently, done the same to them. How funny. Fortunately, I wore foam earplugs and slept right through it all. Since my wife was not wearing earplugs that night, she ended up dealing with the entire situation by herself—all night long—while I slept peacefully. Let's just say that in the morning (when I arose well rested), she was not the happiest camper there.

Advice for reading books on a campout

There seems to be two camps (ha-ha—this was a camping joke, in case you missed it) of people regarding reading. Those that actively read, and those that do not. For the former, reading on a campout is very natural and relaxing to them. Reading on a campout can be a lot of fun if done outdoors and the topic is relaxing and does not require you to think.

Be warned that the avid readers can genuinely escape into another world when reading and might need someone else to watch their kids since kids definitely need to be looked after on campouts.

While my wife and I are not regular readers, when we had little ones that still needed a nap on our campouts, either my wife or I would remain at our campsite, fix a cup of coffee or tea, sit in a comfortable camping chair under our shaded pavilion, and read a favorite book.

And while you might be tempted to read a self-help book or something not so fun, try reading something fictional or biographical or historical. Not something that is going to require you to indeed "think" about it, and then possibly act upon that newfound advice. This is a campout, and it is supposed to be fun!

While there are lots of e-readers available, I like to keep it old school and bring a real physical book. Also, since you often have a lot of glare when reading outside, real books tend to work better that an e-reader for campouts. Quite often (and especially when I am tenting by myself), I will put on my headlamp and read in my tent in my sleeping bag before I go to sleep.

Also, since most people like to feel a sense of accomplishment when they read, make sure to bring a book that follows the typical 10-page chapter format so that you can read an entire chapter in less than 15 minutes. This way, if you need to check on your little one or do some minor unscheduled first aid on an older kid, you will still be at a nice stopping point. With these small-sized chapters, when you get home, you will experience an extra level of satisfaction having been able to read a good number of chapters on the campout. At least, this is how my mind and emotions work.

Come prepared with the right things to help make reading successful though—such as a visor, sunglasses, a comfortable chair, and earplugs (for those that are overly sensitive to noises like I tend to be). If your campsite is super crazy and too noisy to do quality reading at, ask your spouse to hold down the fort while you take 30 minutes and find a more secluded (yet safe) place to read away from everyone.

Why walk?

You absolutely need to take walks. And when I say walks, I truly mean walking. Take in and enjoy every walk that you take on campouts—the ones to the bathroom down the road from your campsite every few hours, the ones to the dumpster, even the ones to the waterfront or playground. Casually stroll and avoid hurrying—you will have time enough for that when you return home from your campout. Some of my favorite campout memories are the leisurely walks that my kids and I have taken. Yes, for hikes, you do need to be more prepared with good shoes, a cell phone, a day pack, water, etc. But I am talking here about just walking. One of the things

we honestly like to do is to walk along the road that runs in front of each campsite of whatever loop or area of the campground we are in. When camping with a large group, this provides a way to stop by and visit the other families. Recently, we did so and our group of people grew from 5 to 15 as we walked around. As we stopped and visited with our fellow campers, many of them decided to join our walk. Over the  years, many of these spontaneous "drop-ins" have resulted in my kids being offered hot chocolate, being invited to play with someone's dog, or even to play a game of ladder golf that's set up in their campsite.

The point is just to walk. Resist any urge that will prevent you from just strolling and enjoying casually walking. Also, this is a way to meet new people—especially any park hosts that live and work at that state park. And if you have a little one, this is a big reason to remember to bring an inexpensive umbrella-style stroller with you. While most strollers do not work so well on the off-road trails, they work on sidewalks and roadways (and thus, on these types of walks).

And finally, these walks are great exercise. And since you, hopefully, are eating well on your campout and possibly having Dutch oven cobbler later, burning a few extra calories is probably a fantastic idea.

Taking hikes

In the previous section when I said to take a walk, I meant to "walk". In this section, when I say take a hike, I am not talking about taking a real bona fide hike. Instead, I am talking about walking on off-road trails around your campsite. This is a fantastic way to get away from all of the man-made things, such as roads, cement, and asphalt, and to categorically enjoy nature while getting some exercise as well.

Most, if not all, state parks have some form of a trail near them or on the premises that are ideal for a "hike." Hike in the morning after you have everything cleaned up from breakfast, with a planned return by lunch. A good 1.5-hour to 2-hour hike would be the goal. For this hike, here are some necessities:

- ☀ Everyone needs a water bottle
- ☀ Trail-appropriate healthy snacks that can easily be packed out
- ☀ Day packs
- ☀ Comfortable shoes with appropriate socks
- ☀ Bug spray and sunscreen
- ☀ Anything else you will need for the next 1.5 to 2 hours
- ☀ Cell phone in case of emergencies

☀ Small, highly portable first aid kit, including mole skin or duct tape for blisters

Before you leave, you need to determine when you will need to get back to your campsite. If the trail starts near your campsite but ends five miles away, you will probably want to consider going part of the way, and then turning around and retracing your steps for the second half.

We made the mistake of not doing this when we went to Robbers Cave in Oklahoma. We were told that the cave was two miles from our campsite. With that information, we headed out, believing we would hike for one hour, spend some time in the cave, and then have a one-hour hike back. Unfortunately, the estimate we had been given was wrong, and it took us almost two hours to get to the cave. Thus, by the time we were done exploring the cave, we did not want to do any additional hiking. Fortunately, we ran into some people we knew who had driven to the cave that were kind enough to offer us a ride back. Thank goodness they did, or we would have missed out on the dinner that was being prepared for us back at camp. The lesson learned here is to look at the trail map or talk to a park ranger about the length of a hike ahead of time.

Try your hand at skipping rocks on a lake

A few years back, we attended my older son's Boy Scout troop Family Campout at Eisenhower State Park near the Texas/Oklahoma border. On Saturday morning, we wandered down to the lakeshore to spend time with other families. While talking to another family, the father and his oldest son started skipping rocks on the lake. For those of you not familiar with skipping rocks, here is how it works. First, you find a small rock the size of a half dollar that is very smooth on one or both sides. Then, you throw it side-armed toward the lake. If you throw it just right, the rock will hit the lake, and then bounce (or skip). Depending on your skill at doing this and the speed of your throw (and the properties of the rock itself), you can get the rock to skip several times.

Back to my story . . . Well, a few minutes later, another family showed up. It turned out the two other dads were friends and were very, very competitive. Within minutes, they had a competition going and were getting their rocks to skip six or more times on a single throw. They were so good that they were getting close to getting their rocks to completely cross the cove we were standing in. The distance had to have been half a football field. These two men were amazing and quickly had a good crowd watching and cheering them on.

As you know by now, I am big on using the principles of Leave No Trace when camping. With that said, I am more than OK with skipping rocks. Now, if this is something you and a large group of people did every single day at the same place, that might be a different story. But as a once-in-while activity, it is just fine.

With that comment made, skipping rocks is an activity that your entire family can participate in. And while some people will struggle to get the rock to skip at all, most people can achieve at least one skip after a few tries. And if you are not already a good rock skipper, this might be something you, as the leader of your crew, practice at home before the campout. This will enable you to be better prepared to help your little ones on the campout to be successful "rock skippers."

Go fishing on your campout

How can you get any more outdoorsy than fishing? Even if you are not a seasoned angler, your kids will love this. With an inexpensive fishing pole, some cheap tackle, and some night crawlers, you will be all set.

If your kids have not fished before, one item to do is teach them how to cast on land away from the water using a fake weighted fish. These are usually hard plastic, flat, and shaped like a fish. As usual, check out the TheKeenCamper.com website for my present recommendations on where to buy these. The goal would be to teach them to cast one of these little guys into a bucket or similar container. Once they get the hang of it (or you determine that they are not going to get the hang of it anytime

soon), you can progress to the water. Many times, this pretend fishing will be all that you do after they decide to move on to the next activity. But without the hassle of hooks and live bait, this should be a low-stress activity for everyone involved.

Regarding actual fishing, as a parent, you need to make a commitment to not lose your joy. Unfortunately, a downside of fishing with kids is that they are continually getting their lines tangled up. If you have the financial ability to have a couple of extra rods and reels ready to go, you can just give them a new one while you work to untangle their mess. This has helped me to keep my stress level down when fishing with my little ones. Most likely, your joy from this activity is going to need to come from the act of you watching your kids fish and not from you fishing. If you want to fish, you will need to come out on your own either later that evening or early the next morning.

When we started camping with my older son in Cub Scouts, his younger sister (by two years) would come with us. While I would set the two of them up with fishing poles in the exact same manner, my daughter was the one that would always catch fish after fish. Unfortunately, after she progressed on to being a teenager, she was no longer interested in fishing anymore. But when she was little, she would even put the worms on the hooks herself after cutting them in half herself as well.

The first time we went fishing at Lake Ray Roberts State Park in Pilot Point, Texas, we did not bring bait. We thought we could easily go to the state park store but found out it had closed after the man who ran it decided to retire. I still find it very odd that a huge state park would close "the" camp store (which was the sole place to get ice, food, gear, and bait) due to one person retiring. But I digress. When we asked the rangers where to get bait, they told us to exit the park and drive across the dam/spillway. They indicated there would be a store that sold bait right on the other side of the dam. They were correct. As soon as we crossed over the dam, on the left-hand side was a beat-up old gas station/convenience store called the "The Dam Store." While my kids did not know at that time about the word *damn*, they got a kick out of telling their mom when they returned home that they had gone to "The Damn Store." My wife was not too thrilled with me about this.

Take a canoe, paddleboat, or kayak out

Unless you live on a lake, going out on the water is a novel experience for your family. And just like many other items in this book, keep in mind that you are doing this *for your family*. With that said, if you take a paddleboat out—

you will be doing all the pedaling. If you take out a canoe—*you* will be doing much of the paddling and steering. The key point I am trying to make is that *you* will be doing all, if not most, of the work. Regardless, it will be a lot of fun.

Let's start with the basics. A paddleboat is probably the most secure one of these three water vehicles (paddleboat, canoe, kayak) that you can take out. It usually can seat four people and possibly a smaller fifth individual as well. The good news is that these do not tip over, even if people decide to stand up. The downsides are they can move slow and require that you pedal since there are no other ways to make it go. Because a lot of public city parks have paddleboats, you will not come away with the same outdoor camping experience that you might be looking for since these quite often are associated with inner-city parks.

Once we were camping at a private ranch in Aubrey, Texas, and the kids asked me to take them out in a paddleboat. What I did not realize was there was so much algae/seaweed in the water that the paddles on the bottom of the boat were ineffective. Instead of moving water, the paddles were just moving this vegetation around. Unfortunately, I only realized this after I was in the middle of the pond. Another thought is to bring another able-bodied adult out with you. Since paddleboats are undeniably designed for two peddlers, this will result in a much more positive experience.

In my opinion, the best option for getting a real outdoor person-powered watercraft experience is a bona fide canoe. First, they feel outdoorsy, and you see them in all the movies about summer camps, etc. The second thing is they sit very high in the water and will glide through the water very nicely. There are a few downsides though. The first being that they can, and will, tip over easily. I always remind others to have three points of contact with the canoe always. This means that at any time, you should have two feet and one hand, or two hands and one foot touching/holding the canoe. Next, do not stand up in a canoe. Let me repeat this—*do not stand up in a canoe*. If you do, you will most likely find yourself in the water. Canoes are also designed with adult canoers in mind—and specifically, *two* of them. They can hold a third adult in the middle (or two little ones) but there will not always be a seat. Thus, the third passenger could find themselves kneeling or sitting in water at the bottom of the canoe. Lastly, the best canoer needs to sit in the back and provide all the muscle and steering if your front-seat paddler is not very skilled.

Before I forget, everyone—including yourself—needs to wear a life jacket for these activities. Regardless of how good of a swimmer you are, unexpected things can happen. There is always a possibility that you could fall into the water and hit your head—knocking you unconscious. While your kids could possibly flip you over, they are probably not going to be able to perform a full-fledged rescue of you. Also, if you are there with little ones and the boat tipped over, you could easily lose sight of one of them. Make sure you are setting a good example and wear your life jacket too. Also, please take the time to adjust the life jackets correctly. There is a strap that usually goes between the legs. If you do not use it, when you fall in the water the life jacket will ride up as high as it can until it can go no further due to your arms. It is very hard to do anything in this position. Therefore, the jacket needs to be snug and all straps, including the crotch one, should be used before even setting foot in a person-powered watercraft.

Finally, kayaks have indisputably taken off and are an option—especially if you can find a two-seated one. Yes, you will need to take your crew out in multiple runs. But kayaks tend not to tip over and are very easy to paddle and steer with a double-ended paddle. While they sit extremely close to the water (and you could get wet from a passing boat's wave or wake), they are very stable. If you have an older child, they can easily take them out solo as well.

Cook and eat outdoors

As I write this section, it almost seems a little silly since you will be camping, which is in the outdoors, so meals will most likely have to be cooked outdoors.

Therefore, my guidance is more for those that are not camping completely out of doors and are possibly using an RV or pop-up-style camper. In these situations, do cook outside as much as the weather permits. After you have prepared your meals, avoid eating them in your tent or the RV. This is one of the reasons that we have a pop-up canopy in our arsenal of camping equipment—so that we can cook and eat outside even if the weather is not the best or possibly even raining.

A friend of ours who is a missionary in Nicaragua commented to me that they cook all their meals outside there. He says that food just tastes better when cooked outside. I would wholeheartedly agree.

Also, think of all the movies and commercials you have watched that romanticize families eating lunch or dinner outside on a Sunday afternoon. There is usually even a long picnic table with a red and white checkerboard tablecloth somewhere in that scene too.

My guidance is simple. First, cook and prepare your meals outside. Second, eat them outside. Even if you do not have a picnic table, you can still huddle together sitting in your camping chairs. With so many families being consistently on-the-go these days, this might be the first time your family has eaten this many meals in a row together in a very long time.

While I have been known to set up our campsite on Friday night, and then head back into town to have a sit-down dinner, I will admit that I probably should not do this. I started this ritual to reward my family for getting the campsite set up when we first arrived. But recently, I had an experience that is now causing me to pause. We were camping with another family and cooked foil wraps and baked potatoes while we setup our campsite. While our dinner was late (around 8 p.m.), we fixed trout (for the adults) and chicken (for the kids) in foil wraps on a charcoal-based fire, reheated baked potatoes that had been pre-cooked at home, and fixed asparagus fresh with "Slap Ya Mama" seasoning. While I honestly do not think the chicken was done any differently than how we would normally do it at home, my kids still talk about how awesome Mr. Sheets' chicken was. In their mind (and mine), food tastes better on a campout—possibly because you typically do not expect it to.

Grill your lunch and cook your dinner in a Dutch oven

While I have devoted an entire chapter to Dutch oven cooking in *The Keen Camper Camping with Kids Volume 2* book, I wanted to reiterate how cooking your dinner in a Dutch oven can significantly take your outdoor camping experience to the next level. Cooking with a heat source that is comprised of coals is not something many people get to experience—not just at home, not ever. That is, unless you have a Dutch oven and regularly cook with one outside at your house. Cooking with a heat source such as charcoal in an oven that is completely outside is a genuine treat.

Also, grilling your lunch is another easy way to get the outdoor experience going. Most people tend to have sliced lunch meats or peanut butter and jelly sandwiches for lunch on a campout. Why not consider firing up the grill and cooking some hot dogs or doing some grilled cheese sandwiches outside in a pie-iron? Make your lunch experience as "outdoorsy" as possible. After cutting up fresh fruit, put a screen cover over it. And if you are a real overachiever, do not grill over your propane gas grill—you can do that at home. Instead, cook your lunch over an open fire. Now, *that* is camping!

Stargazing

It is not typically until I am on a campout that I realize how little of the beautiful nighttime sky that I actually get to see. Living in an urban area, the amount of light pollution has really dimmed down the brightness of the stars. For those of you not familiar with the term *light pollution*, it is where the everyday lighting that our homes and businesses produce (especially the stray light that radiates upward) creates essentially a haze which obscures the brightness of the evening sky. If you are driving toward an urban area and are still several miles out, you can often see the light pollution as a domed area of light over a city.

One of the first campouts I went on as an adult, I looked up into the sky on the way to the restroom and realized how dark, truly dark, the sky was and that the stars looked like shimmery diamonds in the sky. All at once, I could see constellations and clusters of stars that I had not thought of in a long time.

So, take advantage of this blessing and stargaze. At a minimum, get your kids out into an open field and just look at the sky—hopefully with ensuing amazement. Also, today, there are lots of free smartphone apps that, when you point your device to the sky, will overlay a connect-the-dot-style mapping over the constellations. Your kids will absolutely love this. If you want to do it old school, there are also lots of card decks with constellations that you can match up with the sky. Finally, if you have access to a small portable telescope, you can see planets (and the moons of some of those planets) on these campouts. If any of your kids are in a Scouting program, many of them have astronomy-related badges that can be earned via observations made on a campout as well.

What lessons in leading your family can you take away from this aspect of camping?

"Slow It Down"

If you are like most people, your life is full of many activities that all feel like they need to be done now and need to be done quickly. While centered on camping, the core focus of this chapter is to "slow it down." Growing up, you probably heard this mind-set referred to as "don't forget to stop and smell the roses." When you *really* look at the types of items I have listed as outdoor items, they are also slow-speed items as well.

Regardless of whether you are a Type A personality who likes to have things all planned, it is important that once you are doing the activity you have planned so well, that you should take the time to enjoy it fully. This is something I struggle with—especially on campouts. I tend always to be thinking about what is next and sometimes forget to live in the moment.

So how can you apply this to your everyday life, and what good habits can you display and pass on to your kids? First, live in the moment. If you are sitting down for dinner with your family, make the absolute most out of it. Take the time to savor every bite of your food—you could even chew every bite 10 times like the doctors and nutritionists recommend. Ask everyone to stay seated until they are excused. Initiate conversations with each family member about how their day was. For a while, I used to read a chapter out of a book of fables after dinner before we started cleaning up. When I traveled, I would look for folk lore books from other countries. This was initially really hard for my family to have joy about. Almost everyone felt like I was just keeping them from what they needed to be doing and were anxious to get going. Over time, they started to really enjoy this special time together. As a result, we came to believe it was more important to spend time together enjoying delicious food, listening to a story, and then talking about the life lesson conveyed in the book than to quickly hurry through dinner.

So, focus on meals. For at least one meal each day, have your whole family eat together. If breakfast would work better for your family dynamics, then go with that.

Also, focus on bedtimes. As parents, we have lots of things we need to get done once our little ones are in bed. But bedtime is one of the best times to spend quality time with your kids. Each night, take the time to read to each of your kids—even just one short book or a chapter in a longer book for your teenagers. It could be a classic or even a modern-day teen-themed book like The Hunger Games for your older kids. The bottom line is to not rush your kids off to bed. Instead, savor that special time with them. Because before you know it, they will be gone—18 years can fly by quickly.

Next, as my wife and I started to eat healthier foods, we heard of something called the "slow food movement." The basic concept is that it is usually healthier to prepare your foods from scratch versus consuming highly processed, straight-out-of-the-box meals. Equally bad was to make a dish by opening several boxes and cans and mixing everything together. But to make things from scratch takes time. And that is time you could be spending doing other things. I must admit that I somethings struggle with how long it takes us to prepare a meal, but the rewards are huge. First, these meals are the best—much better than what we used to eat. Second, the food is much healthier. And finally, the bonding that is happening between my kids and wife as they cook together is priceless.

What areas in your life are you missing out on "living"? Have you gotten used to having subpar time with your family in order to have more time with them? When you do activities, are you mentally there, or are you occupied with everyday things?

I will end this chapter with a story. Each year, my family makes a 700+ mile trip each way from Texas to Florida to see our family. On the way, we pass through five states. Because of how busy our lives are, we try to make the trip in one day in a single 12-hour shot. We only go to the bathroom when we stop for gas. We only stop for food when we stop for gas. And when we do stop for food, we go through a drive-through and subsequently eat in the car. We have gotten really good at getting there quickly.

A few years ago, we made a similar trip from Dallas to Pigeon Forge, Tennessee, and made the trip in about 15 hours. Once again, we were superstars at not wasting time. But with both trips, what did we miss?

I am sure there were some breathtaking sights along the way that we passed. I am sure there were unique restaurants with hometown specialty dishes. I am sure there were interesting people that we did not get to meet.

Every year, we used to pass by an alligator farm and would say that someday we would need to find a way to stop. But with it being four hours from our destination, we would not. Will we ever stop? Probably not. One year we stopped at a visitor center in a southern Louisiana parish and picked up a welcome packet that talked about the interesting sights in the area. Will we ever stretch out our trip by half a day to stop? Probably not. I think you get the point—we have gotten our trip down to be so efficient that we have eliminated the ability to slow down. And why do we need to do that? Because we have chosen to live so far away from our families and only see them infrequently. And because we try to squeeze our trips in between our already-overscheduled life, we do not have much time.

But on a better note, a few years ago, we did make a change that has helped the quality of our time with our families. We realized that we were taking all this effort to get to Florida, and then were so rushed while we were there trying to see everyone and to relax that it was just not very fun. After a lot of soul-searching, we started finding ways to clear our entire schedule for a solid 3-week time frame during the summer so we could stay in Florida longer. Now, after a week, I fly back to Dallas to tend to our house, pets, and my job. But my wife and kids stay there for three weeks with the car we drove. They stay a few days with one relative, then move to a friend's house on the beach, then on to a family member's house, and so on. While not everyone can do this, there is probably something you can do to lengthen your vacations. For our family, these three weeks of totally slowing down and getting away from everyday life have been a huge blessing. And while I am not able to participate, I am still being blessed by having two weeks to focus on things I have been struggling to find time to do while I am at home by myself.

So, hurry up and slow down!

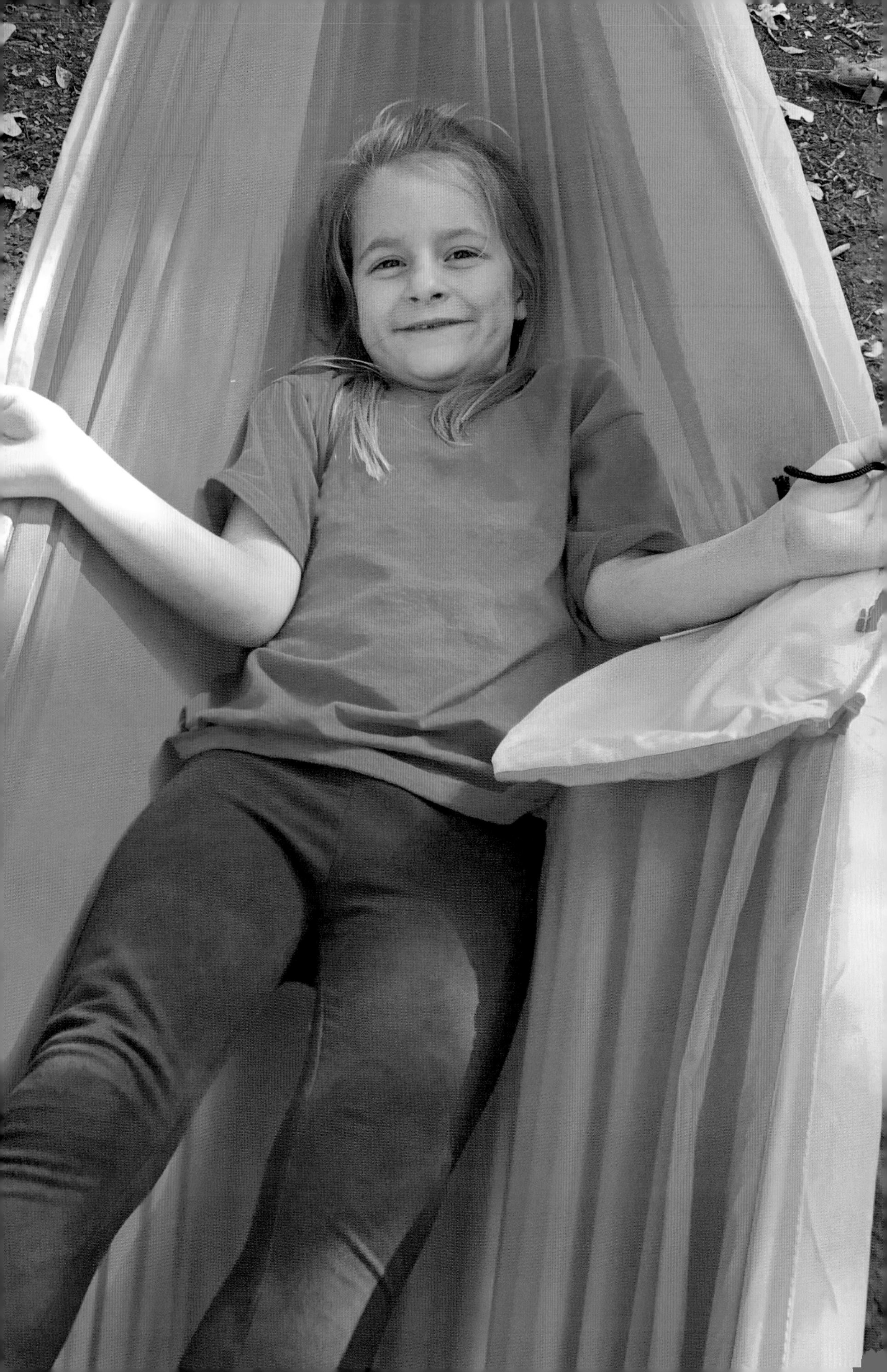

CHAPTER 9

ELECTRONICS, LIGHTING & ELECTRICITY

LED vs incandescent lighting

From my perspective, the two primary advantages of using LED lights are: (1) they essentially do not burn out, and (2) they are extremely energy efficient.

As time goes on, more and more people are becoming more knowledgeable about LED lighting. Ever since lightbulbs were invented in the 1800s, the primary mechanism has been a wire filament. This filament is small enough that when enough electrical current passes through it, it heats up and generates light. Because of the small diameter of the filament, it can break or burn up if enough electricity passes through it in a given time. Another shortcoming of the filament-based incandescent lightbulb is that over 90 percent of the electricity that is used to light the bulb is expended through heat. While at home, you are just wasting electricity; on a campout, you are burning through your batteries faster than necessary since 90 percent of the electric current is being used to produce heat that you do not care about, and only 10 percent is used to create light.

While the benefits of LED lighting are sizeable, a downside is the color rendering. I prefer "soft light" incandescent lightbulbs. Ones that are dialed in with "natural light" or "cool white" color rendering just look very artificial - like the light in a hospital operating room. But since we are camping, does it really matter? I guess that since all artificial light on campouts is fake, I probably should not be concerned.

When I started camping with my kids, I quickly realized that all the other campers' kids had lantern-style flashlights. Wanting my kids to fit in and to be able to play flashlight tag with them, I purchased one for each of my children. What I did not realize was that each of these "toys" used four D batteries. And since kids tend to leave flashlights on when they are done with them, and we were camping a few times per year at that time, we were replacing the batteries twice per year. The cost for the batteries was as much as the flashlight itself. Therefore, each year, I was spending twice the cost of the flashlights on batteries!

Propane vs LED Lanterns

Whether it is family camping or backpack camping, I am always trying to bring the least amount of gear as possible. To do this, I continually ask myself if a specific piece of gear can be used to serve multiple purposes. Sometimes though, it is just easier to squeeze one more thing into the car when a specific piece of gear just does not adequately serve multiple tasks.

For LED lighting, there are some great products that serve multiple purposes. Finding a lighting source that can hang via a hook, has a magnetic edge, can shine a focused beam, can be used as a lantern, and can even be used as a safety alert device, is not hard to do. But when it comes to lighting up an entire campsite, propane is the way to go.

Therefore, do bring a traditional propane-style lantern for outside use. And speaking of the outdoors, please take this as a very strong reminder—do not ever use propane-based products in enclosed areas. The carbon monoxide (CO) that is produced as the propane burns can be deadly. Also, because propane lanterns are extremely hot, and most things in your tent (including the tent itself) will melt or ignite due to the nylon-like material often used. Therefore, only use battery-powered lighting sources in your tent.

But, I would bring an LED lantern as well. As a point of education, a flashlight is intended to direct light in a specific direction using a focused beam. A floodlight is intended to literally flood an area in a single specific direction with light. A lantern is intended to provide 360 degrees of light.

With the advent of LED, there are some great products such as the Coleman ones shown on the previous page that can simulate a real lantern in a safe, non-heat producing, and efficient manner.

Should I bring an actual flashlight and what styles are best?

Regardless of whatever else you bring for lighting, I suggest bringing a traditional handheld flashlight. They are a great source of light and one of the best styles of lighting when searching for items—especially when you are outside in the dark. First, being able to grip a traditional flashlight gives you an extreme amount of control regarding where the light is shining. Second, they provide the ability to have a very focused beam of light. And last, they can be used to defend yourself if you are attacked by another person or an animal—seriously!

The best flashlights these days should have these qualities:

- ☀ Metal case that feels solid and heavy
- ☀ Ability to adjust the focus of the light beam
- ☀ Comfortable grip
- ☀ Easy-to-change batteries
- ☀ LED

Additional features that are nice to have:

- ☀ USB port to charge other devices (and the flashlight itself)
- ☀ Flashing light
- ☀ Side task light
- ☀ The ability to collapse upon itself

Regarding the strength or power, you should shoot to get at least 100 lumens. But do you seriously need 1,000 lumens? Probably not. There are a tremendous variety to choose from these days. Additionally, look at TheKeenCamper.com website for reviews, recommendations, and sources for my present flashlight recommendations.

Finally, avoid getting ones that have a laser pointer. There really are very few uses for a laser pointer while camping, and they can be dangerous. Someone

can experience serious eye damage if not careful, and they can interfere with planes flying overhead as well. Just make your life simpler and avoid flashlights with laser pointers.

Headlamps are not just for miners anymore

I still remember my second campout with my oldest son's Cub Scout pack. We arrived late, and it was well after sunset. When we arrived at Camp Cherokee, we ran into one of the other families from our pack who were also arriving late. We followed them to the campsite on what turned out to be an extremely rough dirt road. As we came around the last bend in the road, I saw what appeared to be a coal miner standing in the middle of the road directing me to turn to the left. I quickly realized it was not a coal miner but instead was one of the other more experienced leaders. I found out later that this gentleman was a very experienced camper and was also the Scoutmaster of his older son's Boy Scout troop. What he already knew (and I would eventually learn) is that headlamps are extremely important in camping and that you quickly get over how you look wearing one.

It used to be that the style was a band that went around your head with another one or two that went across your head with a fairly bulky incandescent light attached to the front. Due to the advent of lightweight LED-based headlamps, there are some great options available to us today—that also look better on you too! They are not only super compact and very unobtrusive, but they also have well-designed embedded battery management technology that ensures a long battery life.

After my oldest son moved into Boy Scouts, we quickly learned a key lesson about headlamps—to have them with you in the car during the drive to the campsite. We typically keep them in one of our pockets or our day pack. Since Boy Scouts tend to arrive at campouts after dark, it is typical for them to set up their tents and shared equipment in the pitch black. No problem for these guys, though. Before they get out of the cars, all but the newest rookies put their headlamps on, and away they go as though it was still daylight. You do not want to make the mistake of packing your headlamp in your main gear bag. If you do, you are going to have to dig through your gear in the dark to find the headlamp that you obviously already needed.

Also, I would suggest a headlamp that is appropriately sized for the person wearing it. While brighter is often better, sometimes the high lumen ones are too bulky for your little ones. In my family, each person who is at least seven years old has their own headlamp.

Regarding features, most can angle up or down. This works especially well when you are wearing a baseball cap and have the headlamp around it. Due to the brim of the hat, you will most likely need to adjust the angle to get the light shining where you need it. When I am walking, I like to have my head up with my light shining on the road 10-15 feet in front of me since I am less concerned about what is directly in front of me.

Do not get ones that are built into your cap brim or snap onto your cap because they do not provide enough flexibility. First, they do not angle up or down, second, they only work while you are wearing your ball cap, and third they require expensive watch-style batteries.

Also, try to avoid models that require you to cycle through limited-value light configurations (such as dual-beam, infrared, and hazard) to get to the one you prefer (such as single-beam).

Recommended styles of tent lighting

Not all tent lighting is created equal. Here are the qualities and features that I look for:

- ☀ Lightweight
- ☀ Can be placed as high in the tent as possible
- ☀ Dimmable
- ☀ LED
- ☀ Light "temperature" can be adjusted from daylight to soft white
- ☀ Controllable from a remote
- ☀ Not built into the tent or poles

Regarding weight, the goal is to find something lightweight enough that it can be hung from the ceiling of your tent. You do not want the weight of anything (in this case, a light or lighting system) to pull on the tent fabric enough to possibly stress and damage your tent. While tent lighting is important, it is not worth damaging your tent. I would suggest a light under eight ounces.

With tent lighting, it is also important to not have shadows. The way to accomplish this is to install your lighting as close to the ceiling of your tent as possible. Lights that run parallel (horizontal) to the tent ceiling create fewer shadows than ones that hang perpendicular (vertical).

The pictures on this page and the previous page show a style that I have successfully used in the past. For my present recommendations, please consult TheKeenCamper. com. I would also suggest that you stay in a continual mode of replacing and upgrading your tent lighting. New models are continually being developed and  released. For example, with the model shown below, the previous model was notorious for the clip of the carabiner breaking off, the internal PCB getting damaged if the unit was dropped, and the light accidentally getting turned on. The new model has resolved these issues. And who knows what features the next model might have—motion detection or an ambient light sensor to determine when it has gotten dark and needs to be turned on. Tent lighting is one of the products that I would not spend too much money on and instead replace it with better models as they are released.

While there are several benefits to LED lighting, one of the ones I like the most is how energy efficient they are. While my goal is not to get frustrated with my kids (and especially not while we are camping and trying to have a great time), I am sometimes challenged when they leave the overhead tent lights on. Therefore, I would suggest that you go ahead and accept that your kids will turn on, and then leave on your tent light in the middle of the day. Just go ahead and accept it and get over it now. No reason to lose your cool over something that you knew was going to happen.

But if your tent lighting is LED based, the batteries will get run down much less quickly. This is probably a good place to remind you to bring spare replacement batteries for when your tent light batteries do need to be replaced. For family camping, I always just replace the batteries and move on. But when my older kids are on Scout campouts, I try not to bail them out. Instead, I let them learn from the mistake of leaving a light on and not having spare batteries.

I also try to shy away from tents with integrated lights. The first reason is that the tent will probably last longer than the lighting system. But when the lights stop working, their weight, wires, and battery holder still need to go around with me to each campout. Now, if you can find a detachable lighting system that was designed to go with a specific tent, that is a different story. I have not yet seen that, however.

Finally, regarding the placement of your tent light, there are good and bad aspects of having the lights at the very highest point in the tent. The good is that the little ones cannot turn them on at their will. The bad news is that these same younger children cannot turn them off without your help, either. Fortunately, with more and more high-tech features being added to camping gear every day, it will not be too long before you can find a setup that is controllable via a remote or your phone. If possible, look for systems where the remote can be clipped or tethered to the tent so that it is easily accessible from the front foyer of your tent but tough to misplace or lose.

Adding lighting to your canopy

I was not quite sure about this one for a while. It always seemed kind of "too much" on the frills side and maybe unnecessary. But I am now a convert. When camping with another dad and his son, we both agreed to bring our coolest gear and really trick out our campsite. We did not coordinate who was bringing what besides who was bringing the food for which meals. Surprisingly, we each brought completely different gear. Since the other dad knew I was bringing my 12x12 canopy, he decided to bring Christmas lights. Since the campsite was really for RVs, there was an electrical outlet. Therefore, he plugged in an extension cord to the outlet on the post, weaved a strand of old-school Christmas lights throughout the truss framework on the edge of the canopy, went back and screwed in the old-style clear incandescent bulbs he had purchased, and then flipped the switch. They looked fantastic!

Here is what I really liked about our impromptu setup. The somewhat haphazardly way the lights were hung gave our campsite (at night) a very laid-back feel. Second, the light provided a warm ambiance and not a sterile one like you can sometimes get from LEDs. Also, the screw-base-style bulbs looked very nostalgic and old school. On the second night, we sat underneath the canopy, and it provided just enough light for our kids (and kids from a neighboring campsite) to play Uno without having a bright high-lumen insect-attracting propane or LED lantern right on top of us. It was great and was a very memorable experience.

Finally, for those instances where you do not have easy access to an electrical outlet, you can either use a portable automotive jump-start charger that has a 120 Volt AC outlet, or you can purchase LED lighting that comes with an optional USB or battery-power source.

Weather radios are a must-have

Tornadoes and other forms of severe weather can strike with little to no warning, and the results can be devastating. During the day, you will probably know if severe weather is coming by atmospheric signs. But at night, you might have almost no warning. A weather radio can help you stay one step ahead of severe weather.

So, what is a weather radio?

A weather radio is any device capable of receiving an NWR broadcast. So what is an NWR broadcast? Via the National Oceanic and Atmospheric Administration (NOAA), a constant stream of updates related to weather and other emergencies is sent out. This stream is referred to as NWR (NOAA Weather Radio). While the focus of this section is on weather-related alerts, alerts could come in regarding abducted children, earthquakes, and even 911 service disruptions. Please note that the term *NWR* is commonly used to refer to the NWR stream as well as radios capable of receiving the NWR stream.

When a natural disaster is on the way, a weather radio can make the difference between life and death.

Please note that weather radios are available in many varieties—some have lots of gee-whiz features including a traditional AM/FM radio, a crank handle to charge it, a solar panel for charging and even USB ports.

While quite a few smartphones can alert you about severe weather that might be approaching, they only do so if they have cell coverage, and if they are charged. On the other hand, a weather radio can receive the appropriate signal almost anywhere and typically do not tend to be uncharged (due to their limited usage, unlike your phone). Who wants to get impacted negatively by a storm because your cell phone's battery died earlier in the day due to texting, phone calls, and app usage—all while on your campout?

With a weather radio, you will have to do a little prep work before using it though. This involves determining what direction the weather typically comes from for the location you will be camping and then entering the codes associated with those areas into your radio. The idea is to get alerts about the weather that is coming toward you and not just the weather that has already arrived. For example, if you know that the severe weather patterns for your area always come from the southwest, then you can specifically enter the codes for the areas southwest of where you will be camping.

What most people typically do is to just turn the radio on, place it somewhere in the campsite, and just forget about. When in the "on" mode, it is perfectly quiet until severe weather comes in (or is in one of the areas programmed into the unit at the beginning of the campout).

Finally, while weather radios are a key piece of camping equipment, they are reasonably affordable.

Using phones & cameras to enhance but not replace the experience

At the time of this writing, except for individuals that are really into photography, the smartphone has become the camera of choice for most people. The quality of the optics and the storage ability is at a high enough level that smartphones can take excellent pictures and videos. And let's face it, it is better to have a picture taken by a less-than-perfect smartphone than to not take a picture at all.

So, I am 100 percent supportive of seeing cell phones out and about on campouts if they are primarily used for taking pictures. And, yes, everyone has their personal preference for what is acceptable or not regarding cell phones on a campout. But here is my recommendation—keep your cell phone with you always for taking pictures and for safety (in case you need to call someone for help). Do have an appropriate protective case and a protective screen (preferably glass) to keep it as protected as possible. Also, if you are going to be near the water, make sure to have a waterproof case or a zippered pouch in case your phone does come into contact with water.

As you take your photos, you can either immediately send them out or just leave that task for later. If you can send them out quickly, that is fine. But do not let a single picture turn into you stopping and updating Facebook or other social media services for the next 10 minutes.

I like to wait until the end of the day when I am in my tent in my sleeping bag to send out my pictures to friends and family. By doing this, the task of dealing with my photos is not hanging over me when I get home, and I have not let my phone become a distraction during the day.

Once when I was camping with a group of Boy Scouts, we had a parent that was texting and e-mailing nonstop. As we walked from place to place, she would walk a few steps behind us using what she could see of us above the top of her phone to guide her. She was extremely skilled at using the rest of us to lead her while she focused on her e-mail and had obviously honed this skill over time. For this woman, it was a tough call because she really needed to do this to keep her non-Scout commitments going while she took time out to camp with us. If I could have provided input to her, I would have suggested that she wait until the end of the evening to do this work so that it would have been less distracting.

About taking pictures, using a smartphone as your camera has quite a few advantages. One of those advantages is that both the date and location can be tagged to each picture. While I knew about this, I had not really thought about it or fully utilized it until a recent Scout trip to West Virginia. Along the way, we stopped and had donuts at Krispy Kreme. Weeks later, I realized that my smartphone tagged where the pictures were taken, including the name of the little city we had stopped at. This enabled me to have more detailed information when I did a write-up on our trip months later. It also allowed me to use it as a reference in case we ever stopped there again on another trip thru that same area. Instead of adding the place to your contact list, you can just take a picture, and then later use the GPS information associated with it to navigate back to that spot.

Leave air mattresses at home

I include this section in this chapter since most air mattresses require that you use electricity (AC or battery) to blow them up. I really do not care for air mattresses, in general, and especially not for campouts. The reason being that there are much-better alternatives. If an air mattress is all that you have available at the time, then bring it on your campout. But please consider working toward a better option down the road. Here are some of the reasons I do not care for air mattresses:

- ☀ They must be inflated. Blowing up an air mattress can take away valuable time with your family. That is, unless you bring an electric pump. Downsides to pumps include the noise they make (yes, I know I am being picky here) and the need for power via batteries or an AC outlet. If using a battery-powered pump, you will be in a world of hurt if those batteries go bad on you. If your pump runs off of AC power, you will need to find an AC outlet.
- ☀ They can be challenging to squeeze through the tent door if they are inflated outside the tent.
- ☀ They take up too much room in a tent.
- ☀ If you are sharing a large air mattress with a least one other person, it can be uncomfortable. It would be like sleeping on an inexpensive, non-baffled waterbed where you feel every move they make, and you tend to slope down toward the middle.
- ☀ Since they are full of air, they are not very warm on a cold weather campout.

☀ There are better solutions, such as a closed cell pads or self-inflating pads.

I guess the bottom line for me is that it just seems so *un-camping*. And finally, if the air mattress has developed a hole since the last time you used it, there are not many options to remedy it short of buying a new one at a nearby store or hoping that duct tape will help.

Several years ago, we were camping with several other families, and one young man was there with his grandfather. The grandfather had both a one-piece cot and a twin-size air mattress that he was trying to fit into a backpacking-style tent. I honestly did not think he would ever make it work. Somehow, he was able to fold, bend, and twist everything until he got both items in the tent. I still do not know how he got it all out on Sunday morning either. And even more interesting (or disturbing), I do not know where his grandson slept—I guess under the cot going diagonally to the cot. It was a *very* small tent.

Electric appliances can take away from the camping experience

Any gadget where there is an equivalent camping version should stay at home (and the camping version brought instead). Here are some examples:

☀ Percolator coffee maker versus an electric version

☀ Campfire with songs versus a radio

☀ Manual can opener (or a P-38/51) versus an electric can opener

☀ Cast-iron skillet versus an electric griddle

☀ Talking (to those who you went camping with) versus a cell phone

Let's take the coffee maker for example. On one of my older son's first Cub Scout campouts, a mom brought a real cappuccino machine, set it on top of a wooden post, and then ran a bright orange extension cord across the field to a nearby electrical outlet. Now, compare that to waking up to the smell of coffee and seeing the coffee percolating in the clear bulb at the top of the pot. Which image seems more appropriate for a campout? And by the way, the percolator (vs drip style) coffee does taste different. I am not saying better or worse—just different. And different is good on a campout. If everything was the same as at home, you might as well have just stayed home.

With all of this said, camping equipment is expensive. Just to make coffee, you need a percolator, a propane stove, and a propane tank. If it is your first campout, by all means, bring whatever equipment you have. The goal at this point is just to get there and camp. Over time, you can work to purchase more "camping" equipment. For example, if want to have grilled cheese sandwiches and do not have your own camping equipment, just bring an electric griddle from home. A simple electric griddle can be used to cook eggs, hamburgers, grilled cheese sandwiches, etc.

But once you get past your first few campouts, try to work toward acquiring more traditional campout equipment so that you can truly enjoy a different "experience" than at home.

Should you bring tablets & laptops on a campout?

I am going to make this one simple. The answer is *no*. That is unless

you absolutely need to run your business and know that you cannot be away from your business an entire weekend. While that is not the case for everyone, this is especially true for families that own their own businesses. For example, I have a friend who we occasionally camp with that runs multiple small companies. At this point in the life of his businesses, he needs to be constantly monitoring things via his electronic devices. But he also does not want to be a bad example to everyone else. He handles the situation by bringing a very nice large tent and proceeds to set up his home office in it—complete with a folding table, chair, and lighting. When he needs to work, he retreats to this "tent office" and closes the tent up. With the tent zipped up (and since it has sufficiently hidden mesh ventilation), he can work without the rest of us even knowing he is in there.

As mentioned in the *"Do Outdoor Stuff"* chapter, we went camping with a family where the father's company was in the final days of a Kickstarter campaign for a board game they were producing. He had his laptop on the picnic table overlooking the road so that he could work as his kids played.

So, in these cases, if you need to bring a laptop or tablet, do so as discreetly as possible and use it for things that are important and not for entertainment. Regarding that, we had this one dad who went camping with our Cub Scout pack that I found had brought a tablet so that he and his son could watch March Madness college basketball games in their tent. I think I would have felt better about this if their tent had had a rainfly so that the other boys did not see them watching college basketball on the campout. Unfortunately, that was not the case.

And lastly, I always tell people do not bring things on a campout if you are going to be upset if they do not return home or if they return home damaged. I think that laptops and tablets fit into that category due to their high cost. Therefore, they should just stay at home. But as always, these are individual decisions that you need to make based on your family's particular situation. I am just offering my thoughts on what I have seen that works best.

Car jump starters are a great choice for a campout power source

I have mentioned the concept of using a car jump starter on a campout in other sections of this book, including the section on using electric fans. The reality is that we have become very dependent on (if not addicted to) electricity and specifically electronic devices. Because of this, on campouts, there are some electric items that we really need like a CPAC machine (to help those with sleep apnea) and some we would prefer, such an air mattress pump or the ability to recharge an electronic device via a USB port. Car jump starters allow you to have access to electricity in your tent without having to run extension cords across your campsite (thus, taking away from the outdoor camping experience and creating trip hazards along the way).

While these devices are intended to help jump-start your car if your car battery has died, they also have the ability to be a portable power source. Today, most come with an assortment of different types of AC and DC power outlets and connectors.

When shopping for one, look for one that has a variety of ports. The best options would be two USB, two 12-Volt DC, two 120V AC, car jumper cables, and an air compressor with a built-in air hose. If possible, it would be great to get one where you can use multiple outlets at once (which is not the case for all of them). I found out mine did not provide this feature when I was camping at the Boy Scout Summit High Adventure Base. I was tenting with our troop's Scoutmaster and offered him the ability to use my charger. What I quickly found out was that when he plugged in his laptop PC to my jump starter, the charging on my USB-based smartphone completely ceased. Unfortunately, I did not initially realize that this is how this unit was designed and messed with it for a couple of hours one night thinking it was a cord or other type or issue.

Also, cord management is a big concern. Unfortunately, to charge my unit, I had to provide my own separate extension cord then find a place to store it (with the charger) when not in use. So, here I am with this super nice and compact car jump starter, and then have to carry (and hopefully not forget) a separate cord.

Also, make sure that the jumper cables can be stored neatly when not in use. Finally, I would suggest that you not remove any items from your unit. Do not remove the hose and accessories for the air compressor and the jumper cables just because you do not think you will use them (since you have not used them in the past). Be smart and be prepared and leave them attached—just in case the unexpected happens. Even if you never end up needing them, maybe someone else you are camping with will.

Wind-up USB chargers

If we are honest with ourselves, it will probably be hard to completely disconnect and not use your smartphone over the weekend. With that said, you are probably going to need access to some form of electrical power to keep your phone charged. For the situations where you do not have access to a traditional electrical outlet or a car jump starter unit, an inexpensive, handheld, crank-handle charger is great to have.

A few things that I like about these. First, they remove your dependency on having to have access to a traditional electrical outlet. And, second, they are kind of neat.

If you do not do this, you will find yourself sitting in your car with it running so you can charge up your phone. You can't be much more "not camping" than this. Also, you are missing critical time that you could be spending with your family and friends. And unless you bring your little ones with you to sit in the car, your kids will most likely not have adequate supervision while you are charging your smartphone either. If it is hot outside, you might have trouble returning to the heat after enjoying your car's A/C too. If this happens, you will want to charge your phone throughout the weekend so that you can enjoy your car's A/C.

If you do not already have a weather radio, several manufacturers sell some with a crank-handle charger. Since that crank is going to be manually turned and possibly by others (like your kids) who are not going to be as careful as you might be, make sure the handle is sturdy. This will be tough, though, since most of the models I have seen only have plastic handles with a plastic hinge. Be careful to note that while some handles look like metal, they are, in fact, chrome-painted plastic.

BioLite stoves use technology to enhance the campout experience

To make this book a little more timeless, I have tried to not reference specific manufacturers and products as much as possible. Instead, I have used the TheKeenCamper.com website for recommendations on specific products. For this section, I need to make a special exception. At the time of this writing,

BioLite is the only company that I know of that is marrying technology and the primitive camping experience in the manner that they do.

Their CampStove and BaseCamp stoves use technology to greatly improve your ability to keep things simple and primitive on a campout. Like how a rocket stove or charcoal chimney works, they have taken that design and put it on steroids. The key design change they made was the inclusion of an electric fan that helps to accelerate the chimney or rocket effect. This fan is connected to an internal battery that initially comes charged. While the battery level is depleted as the fan is used, a built-in thermoelectric generator is powered from the heat the stove generates—creating electricity that replenishes the battery. How neat is that! Presently, they offer two stoves: (1) the small compact CampStove which is intended for backpacking, and (2) the full-size BaseCamp unit. The CampStove works exclusively with small twigs and leaves, and the larger CampStove is powered with twigs and very tiny branches (or other scraps of wood).

Other benefits of these stoves include the generation of almost no smoke and the inclusion of built-in USB ports that can charge your electronic devices or operate an optional USB light for the stove.

Even though campers love these products, BioLite's primary goal was not to make gear for the camping enthusiast. It was to provide smoke-free cooking equipment to families in poorer countries. Across the globe, a huge percentage of individuals (primarily women) still cook over open fires inside their homes every day. The resulting smoke-carried soot is responsible for millions of deaths each year. When BioLite initially started, they only sold the backpacking version of their stove and used the profits from those sales to give free CampStoves to families in need around the world. Due to the huge demand and feedback they received, at the time of this writing, BioLite is now offering the BaseCamp stove to consumers as well.

I love the concept of using high-tech designs to improve the camping experience when done in such a discreet manner. While the backpacking stove is turquoise and yellow, the BaseCamp stove is primarily stainless steel with its simplistic style being very compatible with a simple outdoor image.

What lessons in leading your family can you take away from this aspect of camping?

"Technology as an Enhancer"

This chapter primarily focused on the use of technology on campouts. For those of you not familiar with the term *technology*, it is a scientific invention that was created for a practical purpose. While I really like campouts to have a very old-school feel to them, I do not want to ignore technological advances that *enhance* my family's campout experience. And the word enhance from the preceding sentence is really the key word here. My goal in using technology (whether it be at home in my everyday life or on a campout) is to help me do the things I was already planning on or needing to do, but better.

Let's take an example from this chapter. I need light in my tent. So, why not have the most energy-efficient and most natural-looking lighting that I can? And what does it matter if the electronics inside my LED tent lights are possibly more advanced than that of the computers used to put the first person on the moon? While I am exaggerating here, I am probably not stretching the truth too far. The point is not to avoid technology because it is technology.

So how do you apply this to your everyday life? I will offer some examples of what has worked well for me as I have attempted not to let technology (especially entertainment focused technology) take over my life.

Let's take a smartphone, for instance. If you need the ability to check the weather, to contact a friend, or to get directions on how to get somewhere, smartphones are fantastic. But they come with the hidden cost of lost productivity. Since your smartphone is essentially a portable computer with a display and sound system, you can also use it to watch television shows, to play video games, or to continuously check the news or your e-mail. Do not get me wrong, there are some amazing phone applications that have helped me to keep my brain sharp (think online Scrabble or Luminosity games), but I have also found myself addicted to spending every available moment where I am waiting in line or sitting at a stoplight staying connected. I have found myself checking the news to see what has changed in the world since the last time I looked five minutes ago or checking to see if I have received any new e-mails. I have lost enjoying the moment and being able to let my mind wander, daydream, or just enjoy my surroundings.

The same could be said for a traditional phone. It is essential to have a phone and to stay connected with others, but do you *really* need to have hour-long calls every day with many of your long-distance friends? Yes, it was annoying when there was a cost associated with making long-distance calls, but now that they are free, or essentially free, is this really the *best* way to spend your time?

And remember that whatever you are doing in your life is probably going to set the course for your spouse and children. Set some guidelines in your house. How about a "no-electronics day"? How about no electronics (at all) from 6 p.m.to 10 p.m.? Use your electronics to enhance your life—to make things easier, cheaper, richer, and more efficient. But be careful not to let their associated entertainment aspect consume you.

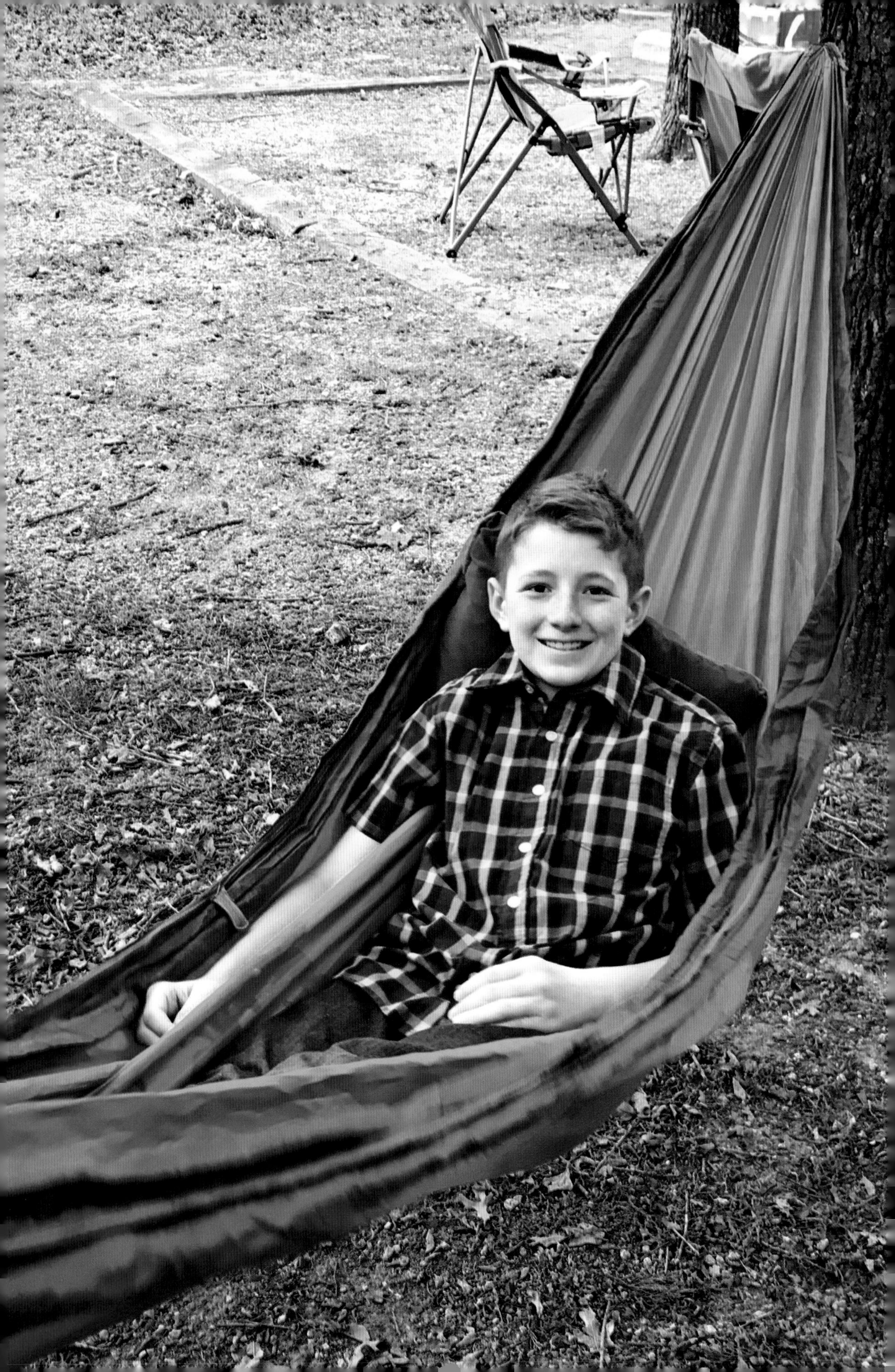

CHAPTER 10

CHAIRS & HAMMOCKS

Camping chairs and a hammock are absolutes

There are many things in life that we tend to take for granted until we do not have them around. Seating is one of those things. When you go to your doctor's office, there are chairs available. When you get home at night, there are chairs and couches. Where you notice the importance of seating is when none is available. You have probably experienced this firsthand when you went to a friend's house for a party or a backyard BBQ. While there was probably enough seating day-to-day for their immediate family, there were not enough chairs for the number of guests in attendance at this party. Standing up for a little while, and even standing up when eating, is OK for a few hours... but not for an entire weekend (such as when you are camping).

While some campsites do have picnic tables, not all do. The worst thing that could happen is that your first campout has the luxury of a picnic table and benches (or if you are camping with another family and they brought an ample number of chairs), and you do not even think about adding seating to your campout packing list for your next campout. Then, on your first campout completely on your own, you realize what you had been taking for granted—acceptable and sufficient seating. While making mistakes is a great way to learn, who wants to learn by not having enough seats for you and your family for an entire weekend?

And if your plan was just to use the campsite's built-in picnic table, who wants to have to sit upright at a picnic table all weekend? Wouldn't it be better to sit in a comfortable fabric chair that conforms to your body and lets you slouch?

Also, how about lying down? While you could do so in your tent, there are a few drawbacks to that. First, you will essentially be inside and will not fully be able to enjoy this natural experience. Second, you will not be able to easily watch your kids responsibly, and third, if it is hot during the day, you do not want to be in a sweltering tent.

So, the best option is to bring a lounge chair or a hammock. A hammock is an affordable option and can be easily hung between two trees. For a little bit more money, you can purchase a freestanding hammock assembly that has its own stand and fits into a storage bag that is just a tad larger than ones used for collapsible camping chairs.

Just remember that standing all weekend or sitting on the ground is no fun.

You need a chair for each of your campers

If you are family camping, you absolutely need to bring a reasonably comfortable and appropriately sized chair for everyone in your group. Even if you are tight on space in the car—period! Even if you need to stack them between the seats or tie them to the roof of your vehicle. Do not "not" take chairs for everyone. With Boy Scout camping, the situation is different, and in that case, just make sure you have a chair for yourself. On these campouts, the youth set up camp in an area separate from the adults and for some reason, they believe it is not cool to bring a chair. On these Boy Scout outings, I used to bring a chair for my older son anyway, but it either never seemed to get used or was not appreciated. Therefore, I stopped bringing one for him unless he specifically asked me to, and this has worked well. When I camp with my other kids and their Cub Scout or American Heritage Girl units, I always bring each of them a chair. So, for family camping, always bring chairs for everyone (even that older son who thinks it is not hip to bring one when he is camping with his fellow Boy Scouts).

While it is not optimal, if space is a real concern, you can bring everyone a small tripod-style seat. Once again, it is better for everyone to have something than nothing. If you do not have enough comfortable full-size chairs and choose to bring a small tripod stool or another small seat for some in your group to use, you (as the parent) will most likely end up using that chair for the duration of the weekend. If you are good with that and have a servant's heart, then go for it. If you do not think you can have joy about that, then do what you need to do to bring everyone equally decent chairs.

On the first campout where I brought my entire family of seven (my wife and me, plus our five children), this whole seating subject caught me off guard. Up until this point, I had camped with individual kids in my family with their Scout units and had always brought two or three chairs, depending on how many of my children came with me. When we camped for the first time as a family of seven, we owned only six camping chairs (which all happened to be the same model in the same color made by the same manufacturer) and a single tripod stool. The morning of our first breakfast, I looked around and saw that all my kids had sat down in the nice chairs (which they did not help to pack or to hurl into the cargo carrier on the roof of the car) but were now all enjoying them. For some reason, I thought that some of the kids (especially the littler ones) would have sat on the tripod-style seat I had brought.

I must be honest and admit that I was somewhat miffed at the situation. Not only was I the last one to get my breakfast (since we served bacon, eggs, and pancakes directly off the grill), but I now had no place to sit except for the small tripod stool I had brought. Although some of my little ones could have shared the big chairs with each other, everyone had decided that they each needed their own big giant chair! Once I got over the disappointment of the situation, I was able to remind myself that I was here for "them" and not for myself.

Also, as pictured on the previous page, you can even spice up your camping chair with a specialized throw. Unlike a typical blanket, these throws are designed with the outdoors in mind. They are super lightweight, stain resistant, and many are even water repellent.

Features to look for in camping chairs

The typical camping chair is one that is fully collapsible, where the four sides all come together into a 6x6x36-inch space when closed and fits into a matching drawstring bag. Most are nonadjustable and have a drink holder in each armrest. That is pretty much it.

If possible, try to buy chairs in darker or bold colors that will not show stains as easily. Also, try to avoid ones where the material looks thin enough that you could see a flashlight beam through them. If they are too thin, they will not hold up well. While many nice ones have the drink holder hole piped with a reinforced rubber/plastic edge, these will eventually crack and break with age (especially if the chairs are stored in your attic between campouts). Also, please see the section elsewhere in this chapter about what type of armrest style to go with.

And while this should go without saying, make sure to try out your chair before buying it. Many of these chairs are designed to be as inexpensive as possible. In fact, many that I have seen appear to have not been engineered or designed for functionality or comfort at all.

If possible, get a chair that has a latch that will keep it locked together when not in use so that you can transport it easily outside of the bag. Try to imagine how easy your chair will be to carry some distance, such as down to the lakeside or to an evening campfire at another campsite. Also, look for a built-in strap that is part of the chair (this is not the strap on the bag) that could make it easier when transporting it within your campsite. These two features (locking and carrying straps) are especially nice when carrying multiple items (like the chairs of your loved ones that, while loving to sit in these chairs, somehow are incapable of carrying them themselves).

Also, avoid chairs with built-in footrests since the kids will use these as a step to get into the chair. The reason to avoid a footrest is twofold. First, the chair could easily tumble forward when your kids try to use it as a step (since it was not intended to be used that way). Second, these footrests will not hold up over time if used as a step and will eventually break. If it is just you that is camping without your children, the footrests are great. They are especially nice if you are short enough such that your feet would normally not touch the ground when your back is against the back of the seat. But since the focus of this book is camping with kids, I do suggest you avoid buying chairs with this feature.

Finally, avoid chairs with silkscreen designs. Depending on the material used for the silk screening, the textile ink can break down over time and become sticky. Because of this, we have had to get rid of all the branded and licensed children's chairs that we had. Additionally, when I camp, I do not want to be constantly reminded of the various sports teams and kids' movies we watch by having to see their logos all over our chairs.

Should you invest in kid-sized chairs for your little ones?

While not too much cheaper than a regular camping chair, many manufacturers make nice small-size camping chairs that are intended for your little ones. One of the biggest benefits is that toddlers can get in and out of these chairs on their own. There are a few downsides that I need to highlight:

* *They tend to want to topple over.* Due to the width and depth, the center of gravity is higher than what you would expect.

Therefore, when your little one decides to stand up in his or her seat, it will tend to topple over. If you could find one where the width and depth are like a standard adult chair, the center of gravity should be lower to the ground. While these would look odd, they would work much better. To date, I have not ever seen one.

- ☀ *They tend to not have drink holders in the armrests.* And if they do, they are not large enough to accommodate most cups.

- ☀ *Larger people cannot sit in them.* This is important in case the child they were intended for decides to sit in one of the adult-size chairs you brought for yourself.

- ☀ *Avoid branded or licensed chairs.* While I do not like branded items in the first place, I do not care for them on campouts when I am trying to get away from my "normal" life. Unfortunately, it is challenging to find non-branded, kid-sized chairs.

Advantages and disadvantages of lounge chairs

Several men that I often camp with have these phenomenal lounge chairs. The reason they have them (and their big benefit) is that they are super comfortable and allow you to fully recline versus having to sit up straight in your chair. The only downsides are cost and portability. They can cost three times as much as comparable quality standard collapsible camping chairs. The second downside is that since they are foldable and not truly collapsible, they take up a considerable amount of space in your vehicle. With that said, I have seen many families that bring RVs with them since they often have more storage space. However, be warned... if you have one for yourself and you bring it on a family campout, you will probably not get a chance to use it since everyone else will want to—especially your spouse! If you like to "kick back and relax" and either do not own or do not want a hammock, these are a great alternative.

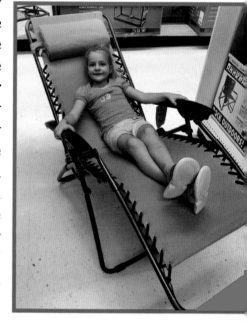

They are especially appropriate for reading since you can keep your head inclined. Also, some styles will lie completely flat, which allows you to use them as a cot as well in your tent. Most that I have seen are considerably more padded than traditional camping chairs as well.

Backpacking and balance chairs

Balance and backpacking chairs are great—for backpacking trips, that is. Otherwise, I would leave them at home when taking a family campout. There are some smart designers out there that have come up with some great chairs that fold up and collapse into almost nothing and are super lightweight. The main issue is they are not very sturdy (at least not sturdy enough for my kids). Second, when not in use, they sit in the dirt since they are meant to be balanced in with your two feet acting as two legs of the chair. This downside to these chairs is typically not obvious when selecting a model at the store since the chair fabric is just sitting on the tile or carpeted floor when not in use. Additionally, if I must concentrate on balancing myself in a less-than-stable chair, it is not a fun "sitting or resting" experience. Also, since I have a slight fear of falling asleep and subsequently falling over in the chair, I never bring mine on a family campout. But for backpacking trips, where size and weight are critical, I would definitely bring one. Also, they are usually not very cheap. In fact, most if not all backpacking related gear tends to be very expensive and at least twice the cost of their non-backpacking equivalent.

Considerations with tripod chairs

Have you ever had someone give you some advice, and while you trusted and respected them, you only halfway trusted their advice? That is what happened to me with the first tripod seat I had in my arsenal of camping gear. My oldest son was going to be camping with a Boy Scout troop other than his own (and without me). Since it was going to be a wilderness survival campout, he wanted to bring as little gear as possible, which meant he did

not want to bring one of our full-size camping chairs. When I spoke to the other boy's dad, he said that his son usually brought a tripod-style seat that he could easily strap onto his backpack. But he warned me about getting one with hollow legs. The problem is that once the thick plastic caps that cover the end of the hollow legs wear down, then the hole at the end of the leg is fully exposed. Once the interior of the leg is open, it will almost immediately sink into the ground (filling up with dirt, mud, or sand). And because these leg end caps are typically not beveled, all the weight is carried on the inside edge of the cap. If placed on a hard surface like a sidewalk, pavement, or cement, this edge can wear down very quickly, leading to the previously closed cap to now become a flap once one of the edges has been cut free.

Unfortunately, finding a tripod chair with solid legs is doggone almost impossible. Finding one with a beveled foot is also challenging but more likely than the solid leg option. A quick fix though is to replace the thin plastic caps with thick tip (cap) intended for a walking cane. While not near as attractive and adding a few more dollars to the overall cost of this style of seat, it does provide a workable solution.

Standardize on the same brand and style of chairs

As with many other things (including camping), I highly recommend standardizing on things if you can. If you already have camping chairs, then, of course, bring and use what you have. Or, if you are borrowing some from friends, proceed along that path and just move on.

But if on the other hand, you are looking to purchase or replace some camping chairs, I suggest that you try to standardize on things. Your inclination might be to buy one chair at a time. Since camping gear is so very seasonal, and since many product lines change or go out of production from year to year, trying to buy more of the same style later may be challenging if not down-right impossible. So, if you can afford to buy the full quantity you need at one time, I highly suggest doing so. Buy chairs for each member of your family that are the same exact style. Having different colors is fine but having different styles is not.

First, if all of the chairs are the same style, you will have less bickering (assuming that your kids bicker) about who gets what chair. If you additionally standardize on the same color, you will eliminate essentially all sources for potentially griping about the chairs. Second, if all the chairs are the same, it will take less time to put them up, take them down, and match them to storage bags since everything is the same. This will also make it easier to train your kids on this aspect of setting up and tearing down your campsite. Otherwise, they will have to learn how to put which specific chair in which specific drawstring storage bag.

Years ago, when I started to buy camping gear, I came across some chairs at Sam's Club that looked great. While these chairs were three times the cost of the low-quality ones you often find at the front of grocery stores near the checkout lanes, they turned out to be the most comfortable camping chairs I had ever sat in. Thus, the higher price was justified. I initially purchased two chairs—one

for me and one for my 7-year-old Cub Scout son. A year later when we started to camp as a family, I went out and bought two more to accommodate my wife and my next two oldest children. But I never went and bought ones for my remaining two kids since I rationalized they were too young and either could not sit up yet or could use the small one we already had. I had already been spending way too much money on camping gear and was trying not to overspend. A couple of years later when I wised up and tried to buy more of them, I was unable to do so. The best that I can tell, it turns out that Sam's must have been the exclusive distributor for this company because once they were no longer carried by Sam's Club, they were nowhere to be found anywhere. In fact, a camping friend of mine had one, and I used to tell him that if he woke up one morning while camping and his chair was missing, not to come looking for me!

Also, as mentioned earlier in this chapter, do not buy chairs that have silk screening on them. This is especially common with children's camping chairs because once the chairs age (or get hot in an attic and age more quickly), the silkscreen ink gets sticky. While this is not the case for all silk screening, we had to throw away two children's chairs due to this.

Armrest issue with some chairs

Several years ago, a major national retail chain of stores was going of business in the Dallas area. Several stores near us had camping chairs dirt-cheap. Even though we were tight on money at the time, we still purchased two of these red, white, and blue patriotic chairs. I quickly found out why this store still had so many available although the rest of the store was devoid of inventory. The issue was the design of the armrest. I have since realized that most camping chairs in this price range also have this same serious design flaw.

As can be seen in the photo below, the front of the armrest is fixed to a metal rod/bracket at the front of the chair. This trapezoidal-shaped armrest/sling has a rubber grommet installed at the opposite end with the vertical chair back rod going through it. The "design," if you can call it a design, is for the rubber to flex and grab the vertical rod as pressure from your arm is put on the armrest. Unfortunately, this is just theory and not reality. The reality is that the rearmost part of the armrest will angle down as the rubber grommet slides down the pole when your arm weights down the armrest. Maybe, the original style of chairs these were copied from worked and had a stiff, firm, rubber grommet—but all the knock-off ones out there now do not.

This is not something that occasionally happened; it happened *every* time. Each time I would put my arm on the armrest it would slip down, thus, essentially leaving me without a usable armrest.

At the time of this purchase, I had not yet heard the following advice, but I wish I had. It is:

"No matter how good of a deal it is, if it is not the right product, then it is not the right product [to buy]."

A few years later, I found a style at Sam's Club (which I mentioned earlier) that did not have this issue. There was a hard stop below this grommet which prevented it from sliding down. This was such an improvement that I immediately donated my existing "bad" chairs to Goodwill. While I did contemplate just throwing them away, I decided that someone might benefit from them. Over the years since then, I have seen that this design flaw is in almost every cheap camping chair that you see at the front of sporting goods, big box, and grocery stores in the spring and summer. My recommendation is to avoid buying them. The only purpose I have seen for them is to reuse the bag for other items such as a bug net frame. Please note the above picture of a chair with a good armrest design.

Keep your chairs clean and sanitary

While everyone has a different threshold on cleanliness, I want to share my thoughts and style. First, I do not bring anything on the campout that I am going to be upset if it does not come home or comes home in a roughed-up shape. After all, it is the outdoors, and your gear is meant to be used. Of course, nobody wants their gear to be abused. So, if I see my kids treating our camping chairs badly (such as standing on them with muddy feet or jumping from one chair to another chair), I will call them out. But life, or more specifically, "camping life," is going to happen. Someone is going to spill an entire cup of hot chocolate in a chair, or someone is going to set a gooey marshmallow intended for a s'more on a chair's armrest. While on the campout, just let it go and do not take much time trying to deal with it. Instead, just enjoy your family and how much fun your kids and you (hopefully) are having.

When you get home, take a very hot wet towel and wipe down and then blot the areas where there are stains. You can probably even use heavy-duty carpet cleaner on these areas as well. The main downsides to using carpet cleaner are:

- ☀ The color may change.
- ☀ You now have chemicals or some amount of residue from them in your camping gear.

Also, refrain from saying too much to your family about these messes. Do not become known as a complainer at the campsite or when you get home. Remember, you are not perfect either, and they are kids. If they acted like you, they would be called "adults," not "kids." And furthermore, look at who is unhappy. It certainly is not the kid that spilled the hot chocolate everywhere; instead, it is most likely you that has lost your joy.

You can certainly ask your kids to help you clean these dirty chairs when you get home. Just make it from the perspective of *"Hey, let's clean the chairs, so they are ready for the next time we go camping and so that bugs are not attracted to them when they are stored between campouts."* To this end, I usually set up all the chairs in the garage when I get home, and then wipe down any issues and clean off all dirt from their feet. A few hours later, everything is usually dry, and I put them away. And, I do so without complaining at anyone.

Buckets with lids provide space–saving inexpensive seating

If you are unsure about investing in camping chairs or are tight on space in your vehicle, an alternative is to use empty 5-gallon buckets as seats.

Here in the Dallas area, when my two sons went to Cub Scout Summer Day Camp (also known as Twilight Camp), they were asked to bring 5-gallon empty buckets (with a lid) like the ones you get at Home Depot. The idea was that as the boys moved around from station to station for their classes, they could carry the bucket with their gear (plus any crafts they built) in it. Then when they got to where they were going, they could also use it as a seat.

What a novel idea! And very affordable too. I have since found out that you can buy a cushioned seat and even a rotating contoured seat as well. You can also get aprons to fit around the bucket for storing small items.

As far as space goes, you can easily stack all your buckets together. This will take up far less space in your car than multiple folding camp chairs. If you decide to stick with the lids that are intended for these buckets, they can be easily stacked together when not in use—thus, reducing the footprint in your car. And when you can afford camping chairs, you can just use the extra buckets around your house as garage trash cans or to put yard tools in, etc.

The difference between a leisure and camping hammock

A leisure hammock is just that. A hammock that is inexpensive and designed to rest in for a brief period and possibly even to take a nap in. A camping hammock is one that is intended to replace your tent on a campout. The advances in camping hammocks are nothing short of unbelievable, with many costing several hundred dollars. I would suggest not bringing one of these on a family campout.

No matter how hard you try to keep your kids from using it, your kids or someone else's kids will want to play in your hammock, and your premium hammock will get damaged. Since the point of being on a family campout is to enjoy your family, I want to once again reiterate to not knowingly bring something that you will get upset about if it gets damaged—such as your expensive camping hammock. These are not meant for family campouts. But for those times that you will be camping with other adults or a Boy Scout troop, these camping hammocks most appropriate.

The main difference with a camping hammock is that they are designed for you to sleep diagonally to the center line that connects the two ends of the hammock. Due to the physics of how this design works, when you sleep diagonally to the center line, you (and the hammock) straighten out. This is compared to you sleeping like a banana in a leisure hammock with both your head and feet higher than your midsection and your bottom, which are sagging down much lower.

Regarding camping hammocks, there are now all sorts of contraptions available such as mesh enclosures to keep bugs and critters out, places to hang lights and fans, and even under-quilts to keep you warmer at night.

Things you should know when letting kids use your hammock

The first thing you need to do is to "let it go," and when I mean "it," I mean the hammock. If it is an inexpensive leisure hammock, go ahead and assume it will be a single-campout-use hammock and that your kids will destroy it (or at least mess it up to the point that it can no longer be used) by the end of the campout. By doing this, you will save yourself a

tremendous amount of stress. And think about it . . . If you took your family out to a fast-food restaurant for lunch, you would easily spend the amount of money that a leisure hammock cost. And the enjoyment of that meal would last less than an hour at most. And if you took your kids to a movie, the enjoyment would only last a few hours, at best. So the cost of an inexpensive leisure hammock in exchange for a weekend of happiness—let's face it, it is worth it. And, yes, while you want to be a good steward of things and would like for it

not to be a one-campout hammock, you need just to let it go. And most importantly, do not try to take it back by deciding partway through your campout that you must "protect that poor defenseless hammock."

Now, with the above said, you do want your kids to be safe. What I have seen is that kids love to get someone in the hammock, have them then pull the two sides across them forming a cocoon, and spin those tucked inside the hammock. I do not know why—but this is just what they like to do. Even when we have new friends camp with us, this is what their kids decide to do as well. It must either be instinct or that they all watched the same internet video of someone doing it.

Here are some precautions that you should take though:

- ☀ Make sure the area underneath the hammock is free of any rocks, branches, or anything that your children could impale themselves on or land on should they either fall out of the hammock or the hammock collapse.

- ☀ Make sure there is an adequate distance on each side of the hammock so that if it is swung wildly back and forth, your child will not rock up against anything.

- ☀ Make sure you have done a top-notch job hanging the hammock and have inspected it properly and that all knots are tight and secure.

- ☀ Make sure all C-clamps and carabiners are fully functional.

- ☀ Validate that none of the ropes or cords are worn or frayed.

Finally, make sure that your kids know your rules for using the hammock. Mine are as follows:

- ☀ Take your shoes off to keep the hammock clean.
- ☀ Do not try to do any loop de loops.
- ☀ Only one person in the hammock when it is being swung wildly. I am fine with two small children or an adult and toddler being in the hammock together if they are only resting in it and not being swung.

I can guarantee that your hammock will be a huge hit with the kids and will be a big highlight from the campout.

Hammocks with collapsible stands

If you have the money and space, then I would purchase and bring a hammock that has a collapsible stand. When collapsed, they are just marginally bigger than the collapsible camping chairs they are modeled after. The benefits of these hammocks are:

- ☀ You do not have to be concerned about finding two trees to hang your hammock between.
- ☀ It is not the type of hammock that your kids will want to abuse (I mean enjoy).
- ☀ You can set up this hammock in the location that is most convenient to you and are not limited by the locations of trees you would hang a traditional hammock from.

Finally, while I have not tried sleeping in one, I suspect if your tent is large enough, you could place it inside your tent in place of your cot.

What lessons in leading your family can you take away from this aspect of camping?

"Adequate Seating"

You are probably still reeling from the fact that you just read an entire chapter on campout "seating." Seating is one of those things that you do not realize how important it is until you no longer have it. So how do you apply this to your everyday life? The answer is, in a very similar manner.

If you can financially afford it, make sure that you have a seat for every member of your family and a reasonable number of guests in your key shared rooms. Assuming you have a dining room or kitchen table, every family member needs their own seat. While this might seem obvious, I grew up in a family where this was not true. While we had the money, for some reason, we only had a table with four chairs although our family had five members. What this meant was that for my entire time living at home, we never had meals at the same table (except for holidays when we used the large 10-person dining room table). Not trying to bad-mouth my parents—they are the best! I am just saying that it would have been better if we could have had a chair for each person.

For your family, TV, or great room, make sure you have enough good seats for everyone too. And when I say *good* seats, I mean ones that you can adequately see the TV from and that have adequate lighting to read by. In our great room, we have seating for eight but relocate one of the chairs if we are watching television and need for everyone to be able to see the screen.

This mind-set really should carry over into everything in your household. As much as possible, everyone should have an adequate place to sleep. While you might have your kids share a bed, make sure they all have at least the equivalent of two-thirds of a twin bed to call their own. And even if it is limited in space, make sure everyone has furniture drawers and closet space to store their clothes. Everyone having their own personal space—whether it is a camping chair or a seat at a kitchen table—is vitally important.

It just seems to better convey that you value all your family members as unique individuals if you have provided individual space for them. Additionally, it also helps your guests feel more welcome knowing that they are not taking someone else's spot either.

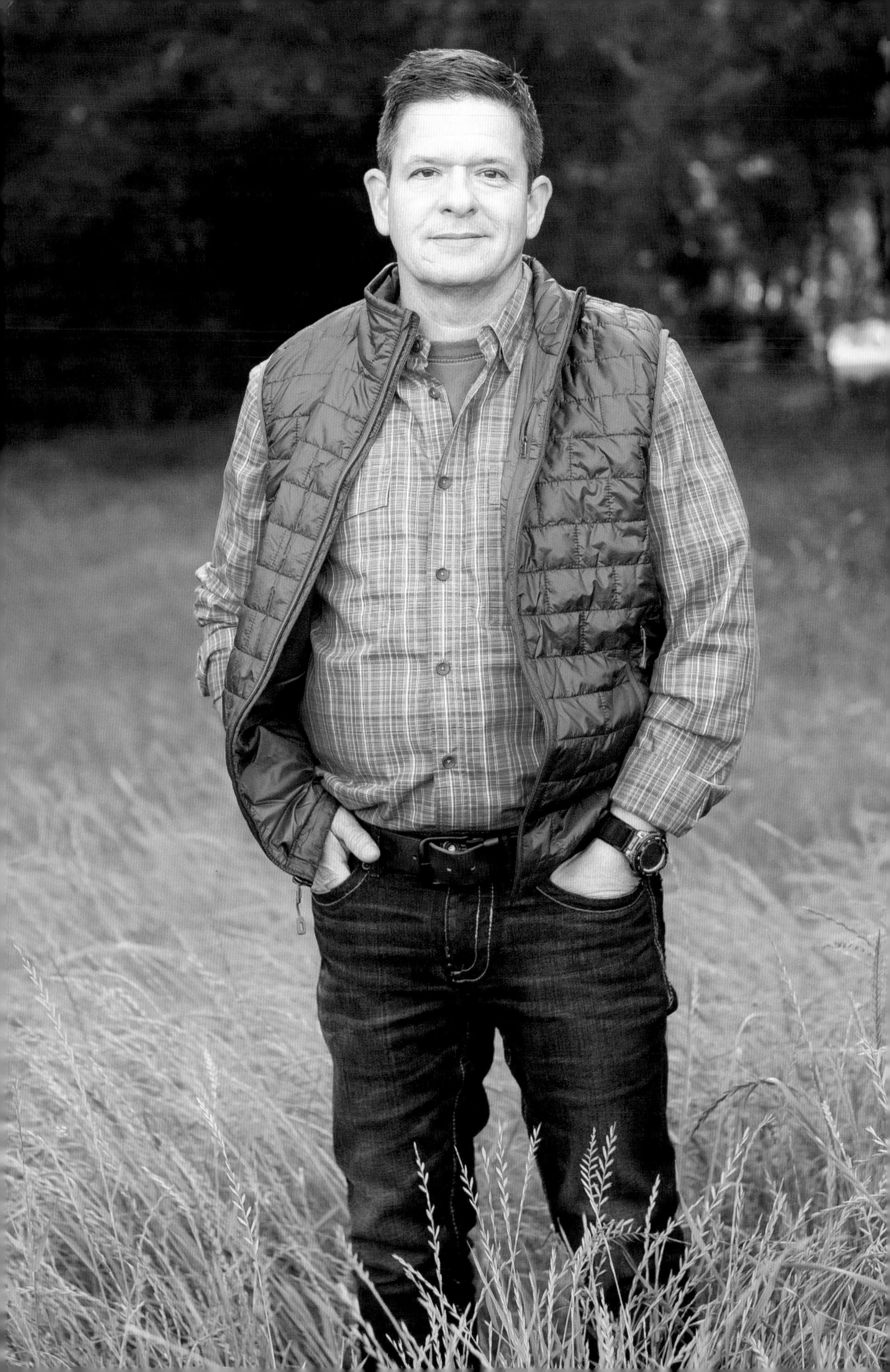

ACKNOWLEDGMENTS

This project was certainly a labor of love. The writing aspect really helped me to get *real* about why I so enjoy camping and even more importantly enjoy helping others get the most out of their experiences. But once the writing was done, the work at times seemed insurmountable. With the support and encouragement of the following people—many who probably didn't even know they were inspiring me behind the scenes—I got through.

My eternal thanks to:

My 8-year old daughter Ainsley who during this time became my camping buddy. Her request for us to go on an "Ainsley & Dad Camping Trip" really inspired me. I came back from it determined to finish this manuscript.

My children Katelyn, Luke, and Everly. Their willingness to go camping helped me switch my focus from how "I" could have great campouts to how "we" could have great campouts. This was a game changer for me.

My son Seth who has always done a fantastic job helping us setup and breakdown our campsite—even when it was not his choice to go camping and cram seven people and all our gear into our SUV.

Pauly Piccirillo author of *The Worm Farming Revolution!* who helped point me in the right direction for how to get a book published. As I transitioned from aspiring writer to a marketer, Pauly's insights were invaluable.

My wonderful wife Joanne who has always been my biggest fan. Her belief in me and her unfailing support has kept me going. At times, her confidence in me was stronger than my own. My forever thanks go out to her for managing everything else so that I could focus on this project.

Continued

My parents George & Lynn Riddle. Besides being great parents, I want to thank whichever one decided to sign me up for Cub Scouts in the third grade. That humble start to becoming an Eagle Scout like my father, lead me to a love for camping and the outdoors. Thanks, Mom & Dad!

Josh Harley who helped me with many of the design decisions regarding The Keen Camper brand, my logo, and encouraging me to invest in copyediting to make sure my book could be the best it could.

Geoffrey Stertz for designing the amazing cover for this book and the rest of the series. Geoffrey was my *go-to guy* for so many of the design choices on this journey. Thanks!

My friend Nathan Sheets who has publically sung my praises to so many and made a such a big deal to others about how much camping knowledge I knew and for being an Eagle Scout. His over-the-top compliments encouraged me to become the person he described (but wasn't quite yet).

God for blessing me with so much and reminding me daily that I am not here on this Earth for myself but instead to focus on helping others.

INDEX